WHY DO PEOPLE NOT SEE THE BIBLE ALIKE?

J. RIDLEY STROOP

GOSPEL ADVOCATE
A TRUSTED NAME SINCE 1855

Gospel Advocate Company
P.O. Box 150
Nashville, Tennessee 37202

Why
DO PEOPLE NOT
SEE THE BIBLE ALIKE
?

"Seek ye Jehovah while he may be found; call ye upon him while he is near: let the wicked forsake his way, and the unrighteous man his thoughts; and let him return unto Jehovah, and he will have mercy upon him; and to our God, for he will abundantly pardon. For my thoughts are not your thoughts, neither are your ways my ways, saith Jehovah. For as the heavens are higher than the earth, so are my ways higher than your ways, and my thoughts than your thoughts" (Isa. 55:6-9).

Author and Publisher
J. RIDLEY STROOP
David Lipscomb College
Nashville 4, Tennessee

Why Do People Not See the Bible Alike?
Gospel Advocate Reprint Library Edition, 2001

© 1949, J. Ridley Stroop

Published by Gospel Advocate Co.
P.O. Box 150, Nashville, TN 37202
www.gospeladvocate.com

ISBN: 0-89225-522-6

TABLE OF CONTENTS

DEDICATION

THIS BOOK is sincerely and prayerfully dedicated to every honest person who is earnestly seeking the truth of his God and whose sincerity inclines him to pause here and pray that what he may glean from the thoughts that follow may lead him more fully into the truth and that he may be guarded against any distracting or misguiding influence that may be hidden among them.

FOREWORD

T HESE lectures are the result of prayerful medita-
tion upon the seriousness of the conditions that are
present with us and in the truth of our God which reveals to us the magnitude of the dangers that exist.
They are addressed to the thinking of each individual
with an appeal for due recognition of his personal responsibility before God. The writer holds the conviction
that the only gateway through which a person may
escape from the thralldom of his own religious error is
a personal interest in the need of his own soul and a
recognition that the real need is to truly sit at Jesus' feet
and hear his word. If one sets his heart to dethrone
himself and to enthrone Jesus as his Lord to rule his
life and to seek the glory of God rather than the praise
of men, remembering the blessings and promises of his
God, he will view the matter with a seriousness that will
lead him to make a frank and honest appraisal of his
ideas and actions by the word of God. In a very real
sense each one must save himself from this crooked
generation (Acts 2:40), which salvation must be
worked out with fear and trembling. (Phil. 2:12)

The purpose of these lectures in dealing with the
question of religious differences is not to place the
blame for the differences upon any individual or church
group. It is rather to make a fair examination of the
matter in the hope that religious people may be encouraged to take a realistic view of conditions and act
in their own personal interest and for the advancement

of the cause they love; and that the people among us who have not accepted the Bible may understand that human failures and not the Bible are responsible for the present religious chaos.

Due to the nature of the question considered in these lectures it is recognized that you, the reader, may not find yourself in full accord with all of the ideas presented. For this reason the writer appeals to your sense of fairness and honesty in dealing with those parts with which you do not agree. Read them and re-read them prayerfully, remembering that they originated in a sincere desire to do you good. Observe that no effort is made to establish any point by quoting human authority. This is an appeal to your intelligence by presenting what appear to be logical conclusions from Bible teaching and from facts easily observed in the field of human experience.

Kindly remember how easy it sometimes becomes to read the wrong meaning into material with which you do not agree, and be charitable to the writer's failure to express the ideas in the better terms that you may have selected.

May God bless your reading.

●

These materials are presented in lecture form as they were prepared for oral presentation and delivered to congregational and radio audiences. Each lecture is followed by questions as an aid to classroom use.

ORIENTATION IN THE QUESTION

WHY Do People Not See the Bible Alike?" is a question that has been frequently asked, and just as frequently has it been answered, if answered at all, in a very casual and impromptu fashion. In fact, it has been considered a mere question of passing conversation. The answers have been mere statements of human opinion, and that without consideration of the major factors in the case. Just why this question has not been considered sufficiently important to deserve study is difficult to understand. It may be due to the fact that those who were more vividly aware of the conditions (those interested in religion but confused by the diversity of ideas) were not qualified to study such a question. Or it may be that the religious people were so buried in their wishful thinking that they refused to recognize the conditions as they exist. Or has it been due to the fact that they have been so busy considering or contending for their own religious ideas that they have failed to get the picture as it is? Regardless of what has caused the neglect, it is the speaker's opinion that the subject deserves most serious study. In fact, the conditions in America today, as well as those in the world about us, demand the study of this question. Reference will be made to some of these conditions as we proceed with the task of developing a common perspective from which to more fully understand the question.

When the question is asked, "Why Do People Not See the Bible Alike?" it seems that the most common thought awakened in the minds of the majority of people is the thought of church or denominational differences. With some people this seems to be the only thought. Some have spent much time in bemoaning the lack of church unity, it being considered the source of serious handicaps to religious progress. This thought has given rise to varied activities. Some people have spent the major part of their time, given to this matter, in an effort to place the blame for the lack of religious unity, while others have made considerable effort to restore unity. In fact, some have been so anxious about the matter, and, failing to be able to restore unity of thought, have concentrated their efforts upon restoring unity of form, which has resulted in various church confederations.

It is true that religious divisions have continued to multiply even at an accelerated rate. According to the religious census, in 1906 there were 191 separate religious bodies in the United States who made report to the Bureau of Census. In 1916, there were 202; in 1926, 215; and in 1936, 256. These figures may not be absolutely accurate due to the failure of some to report; but after reasonable allowance is made for such failure, it is still evident that the doctrines proposing to represent the Bible teachings to the world have become more numerous with the passing of time. This multiplicity of conflicting claims is certainly confusing to anyone who is sincere in his desire to understand the Bible teaching; but the church division today, commonly known as denominationalism, does not appear to be the real cause of the deterioration in our religious life. It is merely a symptom of the trouble.

The considerable effort being made by some religious people to remove this symptom reminds one of the treatment employed by some physicians in their early efforts in dealing with high blood pressure. Their reasoning seems to have been from the standpoint of the physics of the case. Since the blood of the body is enclosed in a system of tubes through which it is pumped by the heart, it appeared to be sensible that the pressure would be reduced if some of the blood were removed. This was tried and some apparent temporary improvement was obtained. However, as soon as the body restored the blood deficiency, the high pressure condition existed again. Thus the physician realized that he was treating only a symptom of the trouble and not the trouble itself. When a friend or relative is ill and the physician calls and discovers that the patient's temperature is 104 degrees, we do not for a moment consider the rise in temperature to be the cause of our friend's being ill. The cause may be the presence of typhoid germs in the intestines, tubercular germs in the lungs, or an abscess on the liver or any of a hundred other things. Suppose the excess temperature were treated as the cause. It might be partly relieved by bathing or using ice, or in some cases removed by some other artificial cooling process. This would be treating the symptom and might be of little or no avail in remedying the trouble. High blood pressure and excess temperature are merely symptoms that something is causing trouble in some part of the human organism and impeding its normal processes. Likewise, the multiplicity of divisions among religious people is merely a symptom of a deeper cause which is sapping the energies and deforming the actions of many so-called Christian people. And so long as efforts are directed primarily at removing the symptom, the results are likely to prove disappointing.

Another symptom of the deep-seated trouble in our religious life is to be found in the large number of variations in the individual interpretations of Bible truths. In our concern over the divisions that have separated religious peoples into the different church groups, it seems that differences among individuals within the groups have been overlooked. The fact is that they are more numerous, and probably more dangerous in some ways, than those known as denominational differences.

The magnitude of such differences is very forcibly illustrated by the answers to the question that has been so repeatedly asked during recent years, "What part should a Christian take in carnal warfare?" With the exception of that group of people who call themselves The Friends, no church group seems to completely agree upon what the answer should be. The answers vary from one extreme to the other, not only among those members who are known as lay members, but also among the leadership, including the clergy. Some say that the Christian should take no part whatsoever in carnal warfare, not even the purchase of a War Saving Stamp, or the collecting of rubber or scrap iron, or the saving of tin cans; while there are others within the same religious body who are insistent upon the idea that the Christian is obligated to do everything within his power. In fact, there are some who call themselves Christians who have insisted that those who have registered as conscientious objectors are merely cowards and derelict of duty. Between these two extremes numerous other answers have been given to the same question. The Bible seems to have merely suggested the question and human opinion has supplied the answers. What a difference there would be in the religious world today if the right answer to this question were fully accepted.

The foregoing question illustrates the range of individual differences. The following questions are given to illustrate the multiplicity of differences and the variety of subjects upon which these differences exist.

> What part should the Christian take in civil government?
> What use should the Christian make of civil law?
> Should a Christian marry a non-Christian?
> What constitutes a just cause for divorce?
> What is adultery?
> What is murder?
> Is it right to dance?
> Is it right to gamble?

What beverages, or to what extent, may a Christian
drink?

Is it necessary for the Christian to attend church
regularly?

How much should one give?

These questions, with many others which these suggest, should indicate that there are more differences
between the individuals within some of the respective
churches than there are between any two church
groups. This, of course, in nowise justifies the division
of Christian people into different groups.

This picture of confusion which the religious people
present to the world would not be complete without the
mention of one other set of differences which further
obscures the truth. This class, though different in
character from the others and one that grows out of a
more generally recognized human weakness, casts its
misleading shadows nevertheless. It is the wide disparity between Christian theory and practice. There
are not only too many people who are failing to practice what they preach, but there are too many who
make the impression that they are not trying to practice
it. As long as carelessness or indifference is shown
toward the basic practices of Christian living, it is no
wonder that a non-church individual will propose to
justify his refusal of the church by the statement, "I
believe in a practical religion." It is true that some may
have adopted this as an excuse. But it is altogether
possible that even when that is the case, it is made to
appear reasonable by the misrepresentation of Bible
teaching in practice. The teaching of Jesus of Nazareth

is the most practical that has ever been provided, being the product of divine wisdom and tailored to suit man's nature and needs. Everyone agrees that the Bible teaches the principle of honesty but the divergence of practice by those who have accepted the teaching distorts the principle until it is not recognizable. Such is the case with other such principles.

Another condition in the life of America today that is crying for attention is the social and moral degeneration. Crime and juvenile delinquency have grown by leaps and bounds during the last few decades. The purity of woman, the honor of motherhood, the sanctity of the home are rapidly deteriorating as a result of increasing freedom in lustful self-indulgence. Our social, industrial, and political conditions had become so alarming before we were faced with the recent national emergency (World War II) that the national as well as local leadership was making appeals to church people to save America. (The war period certainly in no way improved these conditions.) When the public press carries such statements as this, "If the nation is saved, the religious people will have it to do," it evidences the recognition of the fact that religion is practically the only definite and effective restraint upon immorality or guide for moral practices. Such appeals should also sound a warning that church influence over American life generally is on the wane. The condition appears even more serious when we realize that indifference toward religion has increased to the point where more than 50 per cent of the people of the United States have refused to claim any share in religious matters. The influence of this increasing majority should not be underestimated. Its weight, through popularized social customs, is already affecting practices of religious people as well as liberalizing their Biblical interpretations.

The conditions that have been described have been referred to as symptoms. It must be remembered, however, that frequently symptoms become very annoying or even markedly detrimental to the welfare of the patient. They complicate matters by becoming secondary causes and contributing to the seriousness of the case. Thus these conditions are becoming increasingly harmful to the cause of Christianity. These conditions become matters of even greater concern when it is recognized that their influence is being made more effective by the nature of the training being provided for the youth of our land. Our boys and girls are being encouraged to think for themselves, to question all ideas, to accept no teaching except that which is in agreement with the conclusions that result from their own reasoning, and this without being trained to supply themselves with sufficient information with which to reason. Neither have they been taught that sound conclusions can only be reached when the facts employed are unquestionably correct. The situation is further complicated by the practice of placing educational emphasis upon materialistic facts to the neglect of spiritual information. It is just as reasonable to expect a person to build a brick house with concrete blocks as it is to expect one to arrive at a spiritual conclusion through the use of materialistic facts.

Thus educational method and educational content have produced a generation quite unlike those that have preceded it. So instead of accepting the religious ideas of their forebears without allowing the variations in religious opinions to seriously suggest the question of authority, the young people of today with their questioning attitude, their independent spirit, and their materialistic educational content are much more likely to accept the religious inconsistencies of the present as evidence against the Bible teaching as the Word of God and thus void its influence in their lives. The effect of this training of youth upon its religious attitudes, the influence of the growing majority of non-religious people, and the fearful increase in the American population between the ages of one and six years should certainly demand that religious people make an effort to discover the cause of religious troubles so that their efforts at correction may be more intelligently directed.

Since the differences between the various church groups, the differences between individual interpretations, and the disparity between theory and practice are only symptoms of our religious troubles, what are their real causes? This question suggests that when we have found the answer to the question, "Why Do People Not See the Bible Alike?" we shall have, at least in part, also answered the question, "What is the real cause of the religious trouble of today?" Or, speaking in terms of individual Christians, we will know what some of man's most dangerous pitfalls are.

When we think of the matter from this angle, it is evident that the purpose of this study is not for the satisfaction of human curiosity. Neither does it propose to indulge in self-justification by attempting to place the blame for existing conditions upon some person or some church group. So long as such is practiced, so long will the whole matter be misunderstood. On the contrary, if each individual can, for the present, forget the failures of others and honestly seek to think of himself, allowing the light of God's Word to reveal to himself his own weaknesses, we may hope to benefit from this discussion. In reality this should be the approach to all questions which concern man's spiritual life and development. It is true that we are our brother's keeper, but not until we have truly accepted the responsibility for keeping ourselves.

Since the question has been described as one of great importance and since some statements may be made which may appear to be dogmatic, the speaker wishes to make it clear that the ideas which are presented are those which he has gleaned from careful and prayerful Bible study. He in nowise wishes to pose as an authority in the matter. You are not asked to blindly accept the thoughts which are presented but to consider them. No claim is made for infallibility. Also, it should be remembered that God's teaching is divine and we are human. Probably all have limitations that we have not fully recognized. May we all learn to "seek first the

kingdom of God" and recognize our own unrighteousness.

Before we enter into the main body of the discussion,
there are a few basic facts which should be called to
mind. The first, one that is absolutely necessary, is that
Jesus brought one teaching. Jesus declared, "My teaching is not mine, but his that sent me" (John 7:16). A
careful study of Jesus' public sermons, of his private
utterances, of his lessons by the sea and on the moun-
tains, in the temple, and in private conversation, his
parables, miracles, and demonstrations, all agree with
the fact that he brought to those people one teaching.
We never find that Jesus taught one disciple a lesson
and taught another disciple to the contrary. He never
taught one the lesson of loving his neighbor and gave
another the privilege of doing otherwise. Likewise,
we find the disciples in perfect agreement in their
teachings. They taught all men to do the same thing
in order to become Christians, and to practice the same
thing as Christians. Furthermore, the Holy Spirit which
was sent from heaven as a guide for them and a teacher
for them directed them all in the same teaching, and
brought to their remembrance the things which Jesus
had taught (John 14:26; 16:13-14). Other emphasis
is given to the unity of the Bible teaching in Paul's
declaration of the teaching of the grace of God. "For
the grace of God hath appeared, bringing salvation to
all men, instructing us, to the intent that, denying un-
godliness and worldly lusts, we should live soberly and
righteously and godly in this present world" (Titus

2:11-12). Seeing that all these agree to make one teach-ing and that teaching came from God himself, why should it direct one man to do one thing and another man to do differently? It is inconceivable that the same teaching should license one man to drink alcoholic beverages and forbid the other; that it should teach one man that it is his duty to be a full participant in carnal warfare and to forbid another man to have any part in it whatsoever; that it should teach one man one way to become a Christian and the other man another way. Is it not difficult to see how men can be following in such devious paths and all be following the example set by the Lord Jesus Christ?

When people learn a fact they can but agree or else some have not learned it. It is a fact that George Wash-ington was the first president of the United States of America. If people fail to agree on the matter somebody is wrong. That is not saying who is wrong, all could be. That is not saying how much he is wrong. That is not saying how much his ignorance of that fact will cost him. It is simply saying that when people do not agree on the fact, regardless of how many ideas are held, only one can be right. Now it is an indisputable fact that Jesus brought one teaching. No one disputes it. No one wants to dispute it. Our differences are not over what he said. Therefore, when people disagree on any Bible teaching, somebody is wrong and the larger the variety of interpretations from any passage of scripture, the more abundant is the evidence of error. This is not saying who is wrong, why he is wrong, how much he is wrong, nor what he will suffer for it. The fact is, we are probably all wrong on some teaching and believing we are right does not make it so, and accusing others of being wrong does not make us right. How much ignorance God will overlook nobody knows but divine wisdom. Probably one of the greatest tests of our faith in God and love for God lies in our effort to free ourselves from selfish human thinking that we may come to the knowledge of the truth, that we may truly enthrone God to rule in our hearts. We should never forget that this is a personal obligation and that the failure of thousands of others to meet it in nowise changes the matter.

It is true that God's teachings are adjusted to man's needs, conditions, and ability but not to his whims. If there is any semblance of truth in what has just been said, and if we can put any dependence whatsoever in logic, if you and I accept teachings that are inconsistent on any subject, one of us is in the wrong. We may both be wrong.

Recently when these ideas were being presented to a Bible class, a man asked this question, "What is going to happen to those that are in error?" The answer given was, and you will please pardon my bluntness, "That is none of my business. And may I say further, that is none of your business." Just how far a person can digress from God's Word and still be acceptable in his sight I do not know. I know that Jesus said, "Follow me." And I know we are told in Hebrews chapter 5, verse 9, that he is the author of eternal salvation to all them that obey him, but so far as I know God has never assigned unto man, under the teachings of the Lord Jesus Christ, a duty or a privilege of pronouncing the destiny of his fellows. Rather we are taught that God has reserved judgment unto himself (Matt. 7:1; Rom. 14:4). So it is not our business to judge our fellows. Here are some things that are our business.

First, it is our business to study God's Word earnestly, sincerely, and prayerfully, taking every precaution that we do not allow our understanding to be perverted by human ideas and reasoning. Second, it is our business to be diligent in applying the Bible teaching to our daily living that, as far as possible, we "may adorn the doctrine of God our Saviour in all things" (Titus 2:10). Third, it is our business, in so far as we are qualified and have the privilege, to teach God's Word to all that we may, both by precept and example, not being forgetful of the teacher's fearful responsibility.

In speaking of the one teaching I most earnestly desire not to be misunderstood. It is in nowise intended to include only, or mainly, that body of teaching on detailed practices over which many people have come to disagree and which has given rise to both group and individual religious differences, but rather to comprehend especially that teaching that will transform man from a carnal being into a spiritual being. The crying need of the religious world today seems to be a teaching that will beget within man's heart a true faith with all of its virgin power to cleanse from sin and selfishness and to vitalize with a sincere love for God and man.

This is the true germ that produces a new creature and without it church members are brought into a relationship for which they are wholly unprepared. It sometimes appears that we are forgetful of the true nature of what we are trying to accomplish and hence become more interested in having the Word of God, the seed of the kingdom, artificially blossom into "visible results" than to be nurtured into a well-rooted plant that will weather the temptations of time and produce the real fruit of righteousness. It is a much more difficult and dangerous undertaking to produce a blossom or fruit and then grow a healthy plant under it than it is to grow the plant and have the bloom or fruit to come as its natural consequence.

To put the matter another way, the true purpose in Christian teaching is not to cause people to do certain things but rather to cause them to strive to become a certain kind of people, worthy of the name Christian. The practice of a few isolated precepts, artificially motivated, has a very restricted likelihood of producing a spiritual being, but an individual who has been truly converted, having been brought to repentance through a full conviction of the love of God, and having been filled with a love for God and an earnest desire to live a life that will honor God and lead others to magnify his name, will find a reality in the Christian religion and sincerely try to turn away from himself and to do those things that will please his God.

Our dealing with the one teaching should be dominated by the purpose of being and making true Christians who have learned fully that, "it is not in man that walketh to direct his steps" (Jer. 10:23), and have pledged themselves wholeheartedly to "no longer live unto themselves but unto him who for their sakes died and rose again" (II Cor. 5:15), having "crucified the flesh with the passions and the lusts thereof" (Gal. 5:24), and having "put on a heart of compassion, kindness, lowliness, meekness, longsuffering" (Col. 3:12), strive to live "by every word that proceedeth out of the mouth of God" (Matt. 4:4).

The second major fact is that God's teaching is the same today as in the days of Jesus and the apostles. It is a revelation of God himself to man and hence will not change. In the commission, shortly before his ascension, Jesus said to the twelve, "Teaching them to observe all things whatsoever I commanded you: and lo, I am with you always, even unto the end of the world" (Matt. 28:20).

The third fact is that man's nature has remained basically unchanged. Man still loves and hates, rejoices and weeps, cherishes and scorns, covets and spurns, approves and rebukes, learns and forgets, understands and misunderstands. He has the same organic needs, the same drives, the same feelings, etc.

Putting these three facts together we arrive at a fourth by inference. Since God gave one teaching, it is the same today, and man is basically the same today; the causes of man's failure to understand and accept the New Testament teaching today are basically the same as they were in the days of Jesus and the apostles. This being true, we can turn to the New Testament with confidence that we will find the difficulties of the present day relative to understanding the Bible reflected in the lives of the people of that period. Thus we shall proceed to seek our answer from this source.

QUESTIONS ON LECTURE I

1. After what fashion has the question, "Why Do People Not See the Bible Alike?" generally been answered?
2. What conditions may be partly responsible for the failure to consider the question seriously?
3. What seems to demand a study of this question?
4. What is the most common thought awakened in the minds of people by this question?
5. Give evidence that some people have been concerned over the matter.
6. Give evidence of increase in religious differences.
7. Illustrate the ineffectiveness of treating symptoms of our troubles.
8. Name three symptoms of our religious difficulty or illness.
9. Illustrate the magnitude to be found in some of our individual differences.
10. Illustrate the multiplicity of our individual differences.
11. What symptom of religious difficulty may have offered some encouragement for contrasting a "practical" religion with Christianity?
12. What condition in the life of America today is crying for attention?
13. What has indicated the recognition of the fact that religion is the real basis of morality?
14. Name two educational practices that make religious differences a more serious matter today than in former days.
15. When we have answered the question "Why Do People Not See the Bible Alike?" what other question shall we have at least in part answered?

16. Under what conditions may one hope to benefit from this discussion?
17. We are not our brother's keeper until we have accepted what responsibility?
18. What is the author's attitude toward this material and what only does he request?
19. Give evidences that the New Testament holds one teaching.
20. What is evident when people fail to agree on a fact?
21. What is evident when people fail to agree on a Bible truth?
22. What does not make one's being wrong, right?
23. What is probably one of the greatest tests of our faith in God?
24. In what respects are God's teachings adjusted to man and what not?
25. What is not man's business and what is man's business with regard to one who is in error?
26. For what is there a crying need in the religious world today?
27. What is the true germ that produces a new creature?
28. What is the true purpose in Christian teaching?
29. Name the four basic facts given and indicate the one inferred from the other three.

IGNORANCE THE BASIC CAUSE

T HIS is the second in a series of addresses on the subject, "Why Do People Not See the Bible Alike?" The former talk was wholly introductory in nature. Its aim was threefold: to clarify the question, to show its importance, and to state some basic facts which should be kept in mind throughout the discussion. Since these are very essential to the understanding of the materials to be discussed, they are reviewed here briefly.

This question should in no sense be thought of as applying only to those variations in interpretations of Bible teachings which have resulted in denominational differences. It also includes that great host of differences found among the individual members of the various church groups. In reality, the latter probably play a greater part in our daily lives than do the former and are probably more numerous. This being true, it is clear that this is no longer an ecclesiastical question but one which should concern every individual who claims the honor of wearing the name Christian. This presents the question as a personal matter. Hence, it should challenge the thinking of every person who has a sincere desire to live uprightly before God. Of course, the denominational differences, which have their origin in the same human weaknesses, will not be excluded.

These variations in Bible interpretations, both individual and church, are not the primary causes of the
trouble in the religious life of America today, but
merely symptoms. However, if we can discover the real
causes of the symptoms, we will have found the source
of our real difficulty.

The basic facts given are these. Will you kindly keep
them in mind? (1) Jesus brought but one teaching. (2)
That teaching is the same today. (3) Human nature has
not changed basically. (4) The causes of man's failure
to understand and to accept Jesus' teaching in his day
and in the days of the apostles were the same as the
causes of our failure to understand and to accept Jesus'
teaching today.

This last fact provides us with a safe approach to
the study of our question since the New Testament
teaching has not failed to reveal to us the causes of
people's failure to accept the teachings of Jesus and
the apostles. Thus we can turn to the source book of
divine wisdom with confidence that the answer found
there will be correct if we will but accept it. To this
source we shall go. However, since neither Jesus nor
the apostles were ever called upon to answer this
specific question, we may not expect to find a fully
organized answer, nor a list of causes for the varied
ideas about Christian teaching in the early days. Thus
it will be necessary to glean our information from statements of fact and depend upon human organization
for our final answer. Let us pray for wisdom and proceed with care.

Let us apply the question first to the Jewish people. Why did they not agree with and accept the teaching as it was given by Jesus and his apostles? After expressing his anxiety for the Jewish people, and testifying of their zeal, the apostle Paul briefly states the cause of their trouble. "For being ignorant of God's righteousness, and seeking to establish their own, they did not subject themselves to the righteousness of God" (Rom. 10:3). Their failure here is ascribed to ignorance —ignorance of God's righteousness.

We find Jesus also giving recognition to the same weakness shortly before his crucifixion. As he entered Jerusalem in what man has been pleased to name his triumphant entry, he was touched by the conditions that existed and exclaimed, "If thou hadst known in this day, even thou, the things which belong unto peace! but now they are hid from thine eyes" (Luke 19:42). A specific illustration of the fact that ignorance was the basic cause of the Jews' refusal is found in the case of the crucifixion. In his prayer upon the cross our Saviour himself testified unto this when he said, "Father, forgive them; for they know not what they do" (Luke 23:34). Later Peter in his speech in Solomon's porch, after having charged the people with denying and crucifying the Prince of Life, stated, "And now, brethren, I know that in ignorance ye did it, as did also your rulers" (Acts 3:17). Later, in his speech at Antioch and referring to the crucifixion, the apostle Paul said, "For they that dwell in Jerusalem, and their rulers, because they knew him not, nor the voices of the prophets which are read every sabbath, fulfilled them by condemning him" (Acts 13:27). In writing to the Corinthians, referring to both Jewish and Roman rulers, Paul declared, "Which none of the rulers of this world hath known: for had they known it, they would not have crucified the Lord of glory" (I Cor. 2:8). This has probably not been our way of thinking of the crucifixion, but when Jesus said, "For they know not what they do," and Peter, "In ignorance, ye did it," and Paul, "They knew him not," and "Had they known it they would not have crucified the Lord of glory," we can but agree. Probably we have been too quick and too willing to attribute the crucifixion of our Lord to the maliciousness and wickedness of the Jews. In fact, we are probably entirely too quick to attribute the behavior of our fellows to jealousy, or envy, or some other form of wickedness, without looking behind them to find that the basic cause is ignorance.

But before we press this point further, let us consider another case among the Jews. This time it is the personal life of the apostle Paul, formerly Saul of Tarsus. Our recorded history of his life begins with his keeping the garments of those who stoned Stephen (Acts 7:58). From that time to the time of his conversion on the road to Damascus, the central purpose of his life seems to have been the destruction of those who had accepted the teaching of the Lord Jesus Christ. He persecuted Christians from city to city, casting them into prison and giving his word against them when they were put to death (Acts 26:10). To what would we attribute such behavior?   Instead of answering the question ourselves, suppose we let Paul speak for himself. "I thank him that enabled me, even Christ Jesus our Lord, for that he counted me faithful, appointing me to his service; though I was before a blasphemer, and a persecutor, and injurious: howbeit I obtained mercy, because I did it ignorantly in unbelief" (I Tim. 1:12-13). Paul's answer, "Because I did it ignorantly in unbelief." Here Paul is saying that he had refused or failed to believe that Jesus of Nazareth was the Son of God, and thus, refusing this information or truth, he remained in ignorance. Thus, ignorantly he became a blasphemer and a persecutor and injurious. As he declares in his speech before King Agrippa, "I verily thought with myself that I ought to do many things contrary to the name of Jesus of Nazareth" (Acts 26:9). Is this not the case of literally millions of people today —that they are living as they are, ignorantly, because they fail to accept the truth that Jesus of Nazareth is the Son of God? And is it not equally true that hundreds of thousands of people who have confessed Jesus to be the Christ are following practices which they ought not to follow, ignorantly, because they have failed to accept what the Bible teaches on the matter? Let us not forget that our abundance of conflicting ideas and practices is *prima facie* evidence that many are in error.

Before leaving the case of the apostle Paul, there is another statement which should be considered. When he was first brought before the Jewish Council for trial,

he said, "Brethren, I have lived before God in all good
conscience until this day" (Acts 23:1). This statement
includes the period of Paul's life during which he was
persecuting the church; and it simply tells us that while
he was living the life of a blasphemer and a persecutor, he was fully confident that he was doing that
which was right.   Since this was true of the apostle
Paul, could it not also be true of you or me today?
Because I am fully confident that I am right in a matter
should not be accepted as unmistakable evidence that
I am right.   "For I know nothing against myself; yet
am I not hereby justified: but he that judgeth me is
the Lord" (I Cor. 4:4). "For not he that commendeth
himself is approved, but whom the Lord commendeth"
(II Cor. 10:18). Has there not been a time in your
past experience when you felt sure that you were unquestionably right on a matter of fact, but you learned
later that you were altogether wrong?   These things
should warn us to be cautious, and especially so in our
efforts to serve and honor God.

The next case we notice is that of the Sadducees.
They outlined to Jesus the case of a woman who had
been married to seven husbands and then asked the
question, "In the resurrection therefore whose wife
shall she be of the seven? for they all had her.   But
Jesus answered and said unto them, Ye do err, not
knowing the scriptures, nor the power of God" (Matt.
22:28-29). In other words, the difficulty among the
Sadducees was due to ignorance.   They had shown
their ignorance of the scriptures and of the power of

God by asking such a question. I wonder if many of our questions today do not show a similar ignorance of the scriptures and also of the power of God.

The Pharisees also asked a question which displayed their ignorance. "And it came to pass, as he sat at meat in the house, behold, many publicans and sinners came and sat down with Jesus and his disciples. And when the Pharisees saw it, they said unto his disciples, Why eateth your Teacher with the publicans and sinners? But when he heard it, he said, They that are whole have no need of a physician, but they that are sick. But go ye and learn what this meaneth, I desire mercy, and not sacrifice: for I came not to call the righteous, but sinners" (Matt. 9:10-13). In this case, Jesus quotes to them from God's teaching through Hosea (6:6) and plainly shows them that they have failed to understand and that this ignorance is the source of their present error. The New Testament record shows a second rebuke to the Pharisees for their ignorance of this teaching. When Jesus' disciples plucked ears of grain and ate on the sabbath day, the Pharisees charged them with doing that which was unlawful. Then Jesus, answering the charge, said, "But if ye had known what this meaneth, I desire mercy, and not sacrifice, ye would not have condemned the guiltless" (Matt. 12:7). Here we see where ignorance of this teaching had not only led the Pharisees to ask the wrong question, but to condemn the people wrongfully. Could it be possible that our ignorance of some of Jesus' teachings is causing us to unjustly condemn some of our fellows?

Your attention is next called to a case where Jesus condemned the Pharisees along with the scribes for allowing their ignorance to lead them to teach error. "Woe unto you, ye blind guides, that say, Whosover shall swear by the temple, it is nothing; but whosoever shall swear by the gold of the temple, he is a debtor. Ye fools and blind: for which is greater, the gold, or the temple that hath sanctified the gold? And, Whosoever shall swear by the altar, it is nothing; but whosoever shall swear by the gift that is upon it, he is a debtor. Ye blind: for which is greater, the gift, or the altar that sanctifieth the gift?" (Matt. 23:16-19).

Can it be that many of the religious leaders of to-day are having some of the same trouble which Jesus found among the scribes and Pharisees? Are they being led to teach incorrectly because of ignorance? It is not necessary for me to answer this question. It has been answered already. The multiplicity of con-flicting ideas that are taught by the religious leaders of today gives the affirmative answer to this question with far greater emphasis than can be expressed by any human tongue. Are you willing to hear the answer? Are you willing to face the issue? Or do you prefer to go on in your wishful thinking, and with thousands of others trust that someway, somehow, things will turn out all right in the end? Please remember that these statements are not directed at the leadership of any particular church group or denomination. They apply to all, for some of these conditions are to be found among all groups of religious people without exception.

Among the Gentile people, what is given as the basic cause of their failure to accept the apostles' teaching? Paul gives us the answer in warning those Ephesians who had become Christians against living like those who had not become Christians. "This I say therefore, and testify in the Lord, that ye no longer walk as the Gentiles also walk, in the vanity of their mind, being darkened in their understanding, alienated from the life of God, because of the ignorance that is in them, because of the hardening of their heart; who being past feeling gave themselves up to lasciviousness, to work all uncleanness with greediness" (Eph. 4:17-19). And so we see that the fundamental cause of the rejection of God's teaching by the Gentiles is not unlike that found among the Jews, "alienated from the life of God because of the ignorance that is in them because of the hardening of their hearts."

We also find ignorance the source of much difficulty among the disciples. They rebuked those who brought the little children to Jesus. "Then were there brought unto him little children, that he should lay his hands on them, and pray: and the disciples rebuked them. But Jesus said, Suffer the little children, and forbid them not, to come unto me: for to such belongeth the kingdom of heaven" (Matt. 19:13-14). On another occasion, "John said unto him, Teacher, we saw one casting out demons in thy name; and we forbade him, because he followed not us. But Jesus said, Forbid him not: for there is no man who shall do a mighty work in my name, and be able quickly to speak evil of me" (Mark 9:38-39). Should these mistakes not suggest to us the need of being careful that our objections to the practices of others do not have their source in our ignorance rather than in the Word of God? A woman anointed Jesus with the precious ointment in the house of Simon the leper, "But when the disciples saw it, they had indignation, saying, To what purpose is this waste? For this ointment might have been sold for much, and given to the poor. But Jesus perceiving it said unto them, Why trouble ye the woman? for she hath wrought a good work upon me" (Matt. 26:8-10). Do we not likewise, though neglectful or inactive, find ourselves criticising what is being done by others?

The personal questions that have been injected into this discussion in no wise imply that Christians are privileged to do whatever they like by whatever plan they like. On the contrary, the care which we employ in doing the things that Christians are taught to do, and in the way that they are taught to do them, is proof of our childlike faith in our Lord and Master. It is likewise a measure of our love for God.

The Christian warfare was certainly to be directed against the most dangerous enemy of Christianity; so we turn to Paul's statement which sets forth this major objective. "For though we walk in the flesh, we do not war according to the flesh (for the weapons of our warfare are not of the flesh, but mighty before God to the casting down of strongholds); casting down imaginations, and every high thing that is exalted against the knowledge of God, and bringing every thought into captivity to the obedience of Christ" (II Cor. 10:3-5). Observe that the apostle does not say that the weapons of the Christian warfare are to be used in casting down those things that exalt themselves against God, but against the knowledge of God, especially naming the imaginations which are mere constructs of the human mind. The final goal set is the bringing of every thought into captivity to the obedience of Christ. Thus, the Christian warfare, within and without, is directed against ignorance of God's teaching, with emphasis upon the major method, that of teaching by example. The apostle Peter states the matter briefly this way, "For so is the will of God, that by well-doing ye should put to silence the ignorance of foolish men" (I Pet. 2:15). Since these statements were made to Christians, they still apply to Christians. Our greatest enemy is ignorance. And its most dangerous location is within the camp. These statements certainly admonish us that it is our business to learn God's word; that it is our business to do God's will; that it is our business to teach God's will to others that we may banish ignorance and establish the truth.

It might be well to remind ourselves just here that the mere acts of condemning, censuring and criticising are not necessarily teaching. And as peculiar as it may sound at first, merely quoting a statement from God's Word may not be teaching. The speaker has not taught until the hearer has learned. It is the obligation of the teacher to present the idea that is to be taught to the thinking of the one that is being taught in such a way as to make it clear to his understanding that it may find a rightful place in his thinking. A teacher should not be misled by the personal thrill which one often experiences when he speaks with authority, in the belief that the learning accomplished on the part of his hearer is comparable with the satisfaction which he receives from shouting his dogmatic assertions. Neither should the teacher be surprised to find that his hearer has not learned or been taught, even though the statements made have been plain, direct and simple, so far as the speaker is concerned. And the practice of any teacher of becoming so forgetful as to blame his failure upon his hearers by an implication that they are feeble-minded certainly has no place in the teaching process. If so, we surely would have found that the Master Teacher made use of it, for there was one very simple truth which he presented to the disciples over and over again; yet they did not understand. Study the Gospels and see how many times Jesus told his disciples that he would be crucified and would arise from the dead. And, although they had confessed him to be the Christ, the son of the Living God, they had not yet learned the lesson when he was taken down from the cross and placed in the tomb. No, not even when the tomb was found empty did they understand. And the announcement that he had risen from the dead was considered as idle talk. So let us not forget our mission, to put to silence ignorance, not temporarily by brow beating, but permanently by leading our hearers into the light of the truth. And, if they fail to understand the words we say, perhaps they can understand the lives that we live (I Pet. 3:1).

If the thoughts from the New Testament that have been presented have not been distorted, it is evident that the first cause for the differences in the interpretations of Jesus' teaching by the people in his day and the days of the apostles was ignorance. This was the case with the Jewish nation, with Saul of Tarsus, with the Sadducees, with the Pharisees, and with Jesus' own disciples. Is it not the case with us today? The purpose of our warfare is, "casting down imaginations, and every high thing that is exalted against the knowledge of God"; (II Cor. 10:5) "to put to silence the ignorance of foolish men"; (I Pet. 2:15) to be the "pillar and ground of the truth" (I Tim. 3:15).

QUESTIONS ON LECTURE II

1. State the threefold aim of Lecture I.
2. To what two special classes of differences does this question apply?
3. Who should be interested in this question?
4. From what source book, and how, must our question be answered?
5. What was the cause for the Jews rejecting Jesus and what case provides a specific illustration?
6. How does Paul explain his persecution of Christians?
7. What reasons does Paul give before King Agrippa for persecuting Christians?

8. What did Paul say about his life of those days that should warn us against thinking that we are doing right because we have a clear conscience?

9. Who is, and who is not approved, according to Paul's statement to the Corinthians?

10. Of what were the Sadducees ignorant that caused them trouble?

11. Of what teaching were the Pharisees ignorant that caused them to condemn both Jesus and his disciples?

12. What error were the scribes and Pharisees teaching because of their ignorance?

13. What is the unmistakable evidence that some of our leaders today are following in the steps of the Pharisees by teaching error in ignorance?

14. Where are some of these conditions to be found?

15. How does Paul express the trouble among the Gentiles at Ephesus that caused them to reject Christ?

16. Give some of the mistakes of the disciples that resulted from ignorance.

17. What is in nowise implied by the personal questions?

18. Against what is the Christian warfare actually directed?

19. By what means does Peter suggest that we put to silence the ignorance of foolish men?

20. What is our greatest enemy, and where?

21. What are some acts that are sometimes engaged in that are not necessarily teaching?

22. What is the obligation of the teacher?

23. By what should a teacher never be misled?

24. How do so-called teachers sometimes blame their failure upon their hearers?

25. What teaching, that appears simple to us, did Jesus give to his disciples over and over that they were very slow to learn?

26. What was the first cause of differences of interpretations of Jesus' teaching during the New Testament days?

WHY ARE PEOPLE IGNORANT?

IN our study of "Why Do People Not See the Bible Alike?" we have arrived at our first answer, because of ignorance. But, as is true in many cases, to answer one question is to raise another. So the one that confronts us now is, "Why are people ignorant?" Since the charge of ignorance against so many people is rather grave, and, since our use of the word is rather varied, it seems advisable that we clarify the meaning of this term somewhat before continuing with the answer of our question.

There are three words that are in very common usage in our conversation about people: intelligent, educated, and ignorant. The first two, of course, are considered complimentary, the last, derogatory. In popular speech we have generally set them over against each other as contrasting or contradictory terms. This, however, is not necessarily correct. Let us turn to the New Testament teaching for our illustration.

We find it in the case of the apostle Paul. That Paul was an intelligent man no one would call into question. Without that quality he could never have arisen to that place of leadership which he occupied among the Jewish people, would never have been given the best educational advantages of his day, nor would he likely have been selected as the apostle to the Gentiles.

Paul was an educated man. We are told that he was brought up at the feet of the great teacher Gamaliel. In Paul's speech before king Agrippa he pleaded the cause of Christianity with such fluency, earnestness and eloquence that Festus cried out, "Paul thou art mad; thy much learning is turning thee mad." (Acts 26:24) Without question, Paul was an educated man. Yet Paul tells us with his own pen that the blasphemy and persecution in which he engaged were the products of his ignorance. "I did it ignorantly in unbelief" (I Tim. 1:13). Thus the charge of ignorance, as it has been made in this study, is not a reflection upon one's intelligence or upon one's general education. A person may be highly intelligent and exceedingly well educated, but woefully lacking in his understanding of Bible teaching. This is not only true, but as our further study will show, superior intelligence or excellent secular education may become a hindrance to a correct understanding of the scriptures. This, however, is not a neccessary consequence, nor does it in any way condemn those two important human assets.

All people who are ignorant of God's Word may be divided into two general classes: those who have not studied and those who have studied. The first class is by far the larger. It may be further divided into two parts. One part is composed of that great mass of people, more than 50 per cent of the population of America, who have taken no part in Christianity. It is indeed surprising that so many people are willing to reject the offerings of Christianity blindly, without making any effort to understand its teaching. These same people would not think of making a business decision or even a social decision of any moment until the details of the matter were considered. Can it be possible that the lack of sincerity among those who call themselves Christians, shown by their indifference and carelessness, their lack of interest and enthusasim, has caused the plea of Christianity to become so weakened to such a large group of people that it is counted unworthy of their consideration? Can it be that the conflicting interpretations, by their continued multiplication, have become so confusing and bewildering that many people have been discouraged and perplexed by the existing religious conditions that their interest has been chilled into inactivity, and their energies have been fully absorbed by their business and pleasure?

The other people that must be considered in this class (those who have not studied) are among those who call themselves Christians. It is certainly shocking that 75 to 90 per cent of the church people of America must be included in the class of those who have not studied God's Word. This does not mean that none of these people have read the Bible, have attended Sunday Bible school classes, or have listened to preaching; but that they have not studied the Word of God as they have studied other things. It has not been studied for the purpose of making it their rule of practice. What would become of our problems in mathematics if our study of arithmetic had been of the same desultory type as our study of the Bible? Or how different our lives might be if we had studied our Bible as we have our arithmetic, carefully searching for the rules of life and diligently applying them in our activities. As life's problems are more complex and more important, the instruction truly deserves the more careful study. We should not overlook the fact that a Christian is a disciple, and that a disciple is primarily a learner. Hence, to be worthy of the name Christian, one must be a learner. This matter should not be taken lightly. If this estimate has been reasonable, the statement that 75 to 90 per cent of church people have not studied the Bible draws one of the darkest pictures that can be drawn with one short sentence. It is the picture of inconsistency.

The other general class of people that is in ignorance is composed of those who have studied but have failed to understand. Can this be true of an intelligent, educated individual? Well, what has happened can happen. The Jews were both intelligent and educated. Yet Jesus says of them, "Ye search the scriptures, because ye think that in them ye have eternal life; and these are they which bear witness of me; and ye will not come to me, that ye may have life" (John 5:39-40). The old scriptures of which Jesus spoke have been designated as their tutor to bring them to Christ (Gal. 3:24), but the Jews, though intelligent and educated, failed miserably in their understanding.

With this class of people, we do not have a mere failure to understand. On the contrary, it is a case of accepting a misunderstanding. This is a far more serious matter. A man who recognizes that he does not know will not go very far misleading others, and will be teachable himself. But the person who has accepted a misinterpretation and is confident that he knows, is exceedingly difficult to teach, and also may be responsible for leading others into the same error. This is the group to which a major part of our leadership belongs. Remember that this is not a charge of total ignorance, but that among our leadership conflicting ideas are taught on many subjects with such persistence and emphasis that it is evident that many, though they have studied, are yet in ignorance and are leading others into the same darkness.

When a person thinks a thing is what it is not, he is deceived. Deception is a major human weakness, the colored glasses that give the glow to sin which makes it attractive. Deception is the process by which an intelligent man is led to sin. It was through deception that man's trouble began. We find this matter briefly stated by the apostle Paul to the young man Timothy, "And Adam was not beguiled, but the woman being beguiled (deceived) hath fallen into transgression" (I Tim. 2:14). Paul made further reference to the matter in a note of warning to the church at Corinth, "But I fear, lest by any means, as the serpent beguiled Eve in his craftiness, your minds should be corrupted from the simplicity and the purity that is toward Christ" (II Cor. 11:3). This statement implies that the serpent is still employing the same method and warns of the danger of the effectiveness of the method today.

John, speaking of the old serpent, said, "he that is called the Devil and Satan, the deceiver of the whole world" (Rev. 12:9).

Deception is not only the process used by the devil to lead the human family into sin, the one which was successful in the beginning, but it is also the process by which evil men shall grow worse and through which they shall continue to lead people into sin. As Paul states, "But evil men and impostors shall wax worse and worse, deceiving and being deceived" (II Tim. 3:13). Now let us analyze this process somewhat to discover how it works in the lives of men.

Paul admonishes the Ephesians, "That ye put away, as concerning your former manner of life, the old man, that waxeth corrupt after the lusts of deceit" (Eph. 4:22). We see here that the old man of sin became corrupt after, or by following the lust of deceit. What is the meaning of this phrase, "lust of deceit"? By our usage of the word lust, it has come to mean evil desire, but originally it was not so; and the Greek word which it translated, which was used by the apostle, carries no such implication. It is the same word which Jesus used when he said, "I have desired to eat this passover with you before I suffer" (Luke 22:15). The apostle Paul also used it when he said, "But I am in a strait betwixt the two, having the desire to depart and be with Christ" (Phil. 1:23). What determines whether a desire is evil or good? Is it not the nature of the act to which it leads? If the desire leads to an act which brings only good unto oneself and his fellows, it is a good desire. If, on the other hand, it ultimately brings evil to himself or his fellows, it is an evil desire. In the very nature of the case, desires or lusts of deceit are evil. Man only desires that which he thinks or feels for the moment to be good. Frequently his feeling dominates, and though he would agree that the final outcome of the act would not be for the best, his strong desire at the moment gives it a temporary value that outweighs other considerations, and thus blinded, he indulges. If, however, he is deceived by his thinking or feeling, then that which he had adjudged to be good, on the contrary will be evil. Hence, if one's desire grows out of deceit, the thing in some way is not what he thinks it is, and so that which he considers for the moment to be good, when properly evaluated, is sure to be evil.

Here is James's description of the subject, "Let no man say when he is tempted, I am tempted of God; for God cannot be tempted with evil, and he himself tempteth no man: but each man is tempted, when he is drawn away by his own lust, and enticed. Then the lust, when it hath conceived, beareth sin: and the sin, when it is fullgrown, bringeth forth death" (Jas. 1:13-15). The first part of the statement completely clears God of any responsibility for man's sin. The second part places the responsibility upon each individual man. Sin which brings forth death is shown to have its beginning in the process described in these words, "when he is drawn away by his own lust." This does not mean to say that all of man's lusts or desires are evil. But that it is through his evil desires that he is drawn away from that which is good. To illustrate, let us consider the sin of adultery, or fornication. What leads one to such a practice? Is it not that he has assigned for the moment a greater value to the enjoyment of a few minutes of fleshly indulgence than he has to decency and uprightness and respectability before God and man? Did he not think things were what they were not? Was it not a lust of deceit? What about the boy who never has drunk whiskey going out with his gang and getting drunk? He hates the taste of whiskey and also the life of a drunkard. How is he deceived? Why does he even momentarily desire the drink? He does not, but he wants to be one of the gang. He wants to be a regular fellow and his momentary desire is so strong that he pays the price. And what a price!

Since we have seen that only evil desires draw one away from God and into sin, that these evil desires are the product of deception, and that all sin originates this way, now we want to know through what avenue, means or process deception works. We read from Hebrews, "Take heed, brethren, lest haply there shall be in any one of you an evil heart of unbelief, in falling away from the living God: but exhort one another day by day, so long as it is called To-day; lest any one of you be hardened by the deceitfulness of sin" (Heb. 3:12-13). Here we learn that it is a hardening process, "lest any one of you be hardened by the deceitfulness of sin." Now for the meaning of this expression let us

examine the context carefully. First, we observe that
the real warning or admonition being given here is a
warning against unbelief. "Take heed, brethren, lest
haply there shall be in any one of you an evil heart
of unbelief, in falling away from the living God."
Second, we find the example used to impress the warning is the case of the Israelites whose hearts were hardened in the wilderness. "Wherefore, even as the Holy
Spirit saith, To-day if ye shall hear his voice, Harden
not your hearts, as in the provocation, Like as in the
day of the trial in the wilderness, Where your fathers
tried me by proving me, and saw my works forty
years" (Heb. 3:7-9). Third, "And we see that they were
not able to enter in because of unbelief" (Heb. 3:19).

Thus the evil heart of unbelief in the Israelites was
due to the hardening of their hearts so that they became impervious to the Word of God. The speaker
warns that the deceitfulness of sin will do just this.
Through this process of hardening the heart the deceitfulness of sin gnaws at the very tap root of spiritual life
by blinding one to the truth by one's own desires
for that which looks good and is not.

Before we leave our analysis, let us examine the case
of the first sin. The first task of the serpent was to
deceive the woman. For until she was deceived, she
had no desire that would draw her away. But when
she was fully deceived, and had come to believe that
she would not die, but would be as God, knowing good
and evil, her desire was well formed and led her to act.
The brief description is graphic. "And when the woman

saw that the tree was good for food, and that it was a delight to the eye, and that the tree was to be desired to make one wise, she took of the fruit thereof and did eat" (Gen. 3:6). Her heart was hardened by the deceitfulness of sin and her belief in God had become disbelief.

Is it not also true that Jesus' temptation was without power because he was without the lust of deceit?

That the danger of sin lies in its power to deceive is especially illustrated by the New Testament teaching on the danger of riches. "And Jesus said unto his disciples, Verily I say unto you, It is hard for a rich man to enter into the kingdom of heaven. And again I say unto you, It is easier for a camel to go through a needle's eye, than for a rich man to enter into the kingdom of God" (Matt. 19:23-24). Also, "No man can serve two masters: for either he will hate the one, and love the other; or else he will hold to one, and despise the other. Ye cannot serve God and mammon" (Matt. 6:24). Paul declared, "But they that are minded to be rich fall into a temptation and a snare and many foolish and hurtful lusts, such as drown men in destruction and perdition. For the love of money is a root of all kinds of evil: which some reaching after have been led astray from the faith, and have pierced themselves through with many sorrows" (I Tim. 6:9-10). These quotations show the great danger in wealth. The last also indicates wherein the danger lies, "many foolish and hurtful lusts," "lead astray from the faith." Jesus describes this power of riches in his explanation of his parable of the sower. "And he that was sown among the thorns, this is he that heareth the word; and the care of the world, and the deceitfulness of riches, choke the word, and he becometh unfruitful" (Matt. 13:22). The power of riches to lead astray lies in their power to deceive. There is nothing more deceitful than riches, since by the use of them so many things can be obtained which men desire; and the wider the range of human desires that it may satisfy, the greater is its power deception, and the greater its danger in leading man astray.

We sometimes hear a speaker say that sin has nothing to offer. This will only be true in the case of the man who is well fortified against its deceptive values. Whenever sin proposes to satisfy our desire, it is offering us something, real or unreal, and when the time comes that it offers us nothing, we will no longer follow its practices. Then let us not forget that the appeal of any temptation to us is measured directly by our desires relative to it, and that our desires relative to it are determined largely, if not wholly, by our scale of relative values which function in our daily living. Theoretical values which we may have set may not protect us, but those that have become a part of our real life will. A theoretical Christianity may aid but little, but a sincere Christian realism is the shield of faith that will quench all the fiery darts of the evil one.

In his description of the sweeping influence with which the lawless one would come, Paul tells us of man's failure that leaves him open to the power of deception. "And with all deceit of unrighteousness for them that perish; because they received not the love of the truth, that they might be saved" (II Thess. 2:10). The "deceit of unrighteousness" has its power with those who receive not "the love of the truth." It is not enough to receive the truth or accept a portion of the truth; one must have the love of the truth. This does not mean love and receive what some man teaches as the truth, but love the truth. Every man who loves the truth will study for himself, especially since so many conflicting ideas are being taught for the truth. And not only so, but he will find joy in following the truth. Unless the truth brings him some joy, he will not love it.

After instructing Titus to admonish the people "to speak evil of no man, not to be contentious, to be gentle, showing all meekness toward all men," (Titus 3:2) Paul adds this reason, "For we also once were foolish, disobedient, deceived, serving divers lusts and pleasures, living in malice and envy, hateful, hating one another" (Titus 3:3). Here it appears that Paul is describing the condition of himself and Titus and probably many others before they came to the knowledge of the truth. We have already learned that Paul persecuted and blasphemed ignorantly, but conscientiously, which implied that he was deceived. Now he tells us that he was deceived. He likewise implies that the people whom Titus would teach would be troubled with the same condition.

Paul also shows deception to be the root of the

trouble among the Galatians when he says, "O foolish Galatians, who did bewitch you, before whose eyes Jesus Christ was openly set forth crucified?" (Gal. 3:1). So effective had the deception been that Paul uses the term "bewitch," attributing to it superhuman power.

In our examination of the question, "Why Are People Ignorant of God's Word?" we have found that it is not due to lack of intelligence, nor to lack of general education. Neither can it be explained by the failure to study, though this may play an important part. The real source of ignorance is deception. It was through deception that Eve was led to misunderstand. It was deception that Paul feared among the Corinthians. Deception was pointed out to the Ephesians as the cause of their former corruption. The warning to the Galatians was against the deception that was at work among them. In fact, deception is the devil's own method and also the forces through which evil men become worse and worse. James has shown us that man is led into sin by his own lust and we have seen that a lust that leads astray is a deceitful lust, and that the power of sin is measured by its power to deceive. Even Saul of Tarsus followed his ignorance because he was deceived. Do we not have here the answer to that puzzling question that has confronted every thinking individual who has been willing to see religious conditions as they are? The question is, "Why do people who are equally intelligent, equally well educated, equally sincere, equally respected, and equally spiritual, teach ideas that are diametrically opposite?" (Sometimes they are leaders of church groups or denominations, and sometimes leaders within church groups.) Yes, this glaring inconsistency is unmistakable evidence that our leaders are suffering from this common human weakness, deception; and there is more likelihood that both sides of a division are wrong than that both are right. These statements are not made to inspire distrust in our leadership, but with the hope that some may be aroused to the great need for more prayerful individual study of God's Word.

QUESTIONS ON LECTURE III

1. Show by Bible illustration that the word "ignorant" is not necessarily in opposition to "intelligent" or "educated."
2. Those who were ignorant of God's Word may be divided into what two general classes?
3. Describe the people who make up the first general class.
4. To be worthy of the name "Christian" or "disciple" what should one be?
5. How do we know that the Jews though intelligent and educated studied God's Word and yet remained ignorant?
6. What is worse with this class of people than the mere failure to understand? Why?
7. Give evidences that deception is the process by which an intelligent man is led to sin.
8. By what had the former life of the Ephesians been made corrupt?
9. Show that the word "lust" does not necessarily always mean something bad but that the "lust of deceit" does.
10. Give James's picture of how sin develops in man's life.
11. How do we know that James was talking about the lust of deceit?
12. Show how lust causes the young man who does not like whiskey to drink it.

13. Through what kind of process does deceitfulness work?
14. This hardening process finally results in what?
15. Illustrate this process by the first sin.
16. Wherein lies the great danger of riches?
17. What evidence would you offer against the statement that sin has nothing to offer a man?
18. What is the true shield of faith?
19. With whom does the deceit of unrighteousness have its power?
20. What is necessary in order for one to love the truth?
21. We have already learned that Paul persecuted Christians ignorantly. What further explanation does he give?
22. What is the real source of ignorance among those who have studied?
23. Summarize the evidences.
24. What evidence would you offer that our leadership is suffering from deception.

HOW HAVE SO MANY PEOPLE COME TO BE DECEIVED?

I N our consideration of the question, "Why Do People Not See the Bible Alike?" today we have assumed that since the teaching is the same, and human nature has not changed, its cause is basically the same as that which was responsible for the varied opinions held by the people of Jesus' day and the days of the apostles. We have examined the New Testament scriptures and learned from those who wrote by inspiration that the cause of the varied ideas about Jesus and his teaching was ignorance. Accepting ignorance as the first answer to our question, we have proceeded with our study by answering a second question, which naturally arose upon the answer of the first. Since the Bible has been the most popular book that has ever been produced, having been published in more different languages and having been sold in far larger numbers, why do we have such widespread ignorance of its teaching? The causes named in answer to this question are two. Though the Bible has been extensively produced, and the sales have been high, it has not been studied by a very large percentage of the people. The cause, however, which is of more far-reaching importance and which is possibly partly responsible for the lack of study is the ease with which man may become deceived. We have found deception to be one of man's greatest weaknesses, the one process employed by Satan to lead man away from that which is right, the main door through which sin has made its entrance into human practices.

Lest someone should think that these important statements have not been sufficiently established, it seems altogether proper that more attention be given to the matter to make sure that our answer is correct. Probably one of the greatest evidences of the universal prevalence of this weakness and the serious danger which accompanies it is to be found in the frequency with which the New Testament teachings warn against it. It is doubtful that any human failing has ever been more universally discussed than has deception. Almost every writer of the New Testament sounds some warning against being deceived. In fact, it is to be found in almost every book of the New Testament. It is probably warned against in more different forms of expressions than are used in any other case. Has it been given a similar emphasis in our study and teaching? It would, of course, become tedious if time were taken here to present all of the details, but sufficient time must be taken to cause us to realize that one of our greatest personal dangers is inherent in this element of our own nature.

Jesus was keenly aware of this human failing and gave many warnings against it. He knew that the people were going to misunderstand his mission. So in the first part of his wonderful sermon on the mount

Jesus admonished, "Think not that I came to destroy the law or the prophets: I came not to destroy, but to fulfil" (Matt. 5:17). Upon another occasion he warned, "Think not that I came to send peace on the earth: I came not to send peace, but a sword" (Matt. 10:34). How true were his statements. Many of the Jews to whom he addressed the first one were never able to shake the blindness which came with their deceitful thinking. And many of his disciples, to whom he addressed the second one, are still confusing heavenly peace with earthly peace. Jesus likewise showed how this deceived thinking would cause other difficulties by leading people into practices that should not be followed. "And in praying use not vain repetitions, as the Gentiles do: for they think that they shall be heard for their much speaking" (Matt. 6:7). Take heed that no man lead you astray (or mislead you) is another form of the warning given by Jesus (Matt. 24:5). It is also used by John (I John 3:7). Similarly Paul admonished, "Let no man deceive you with empty words" (Eph. 5:6). "Let no man beguile you in any wise" (II Thess. 2:3).

Another form used to express this warning is, "Be not deceived." Paul warned the Galatians (6:7), "Be not deceived; God is not mocked." He wrote, "Or know ye not that the unrighteous shall not inherit the kingdom of God? Be not deceived: neither fornicators, nor idolaters, nor adulterers, nor effeminate, nor abusers of themselves with men, nor thieves, nor covetous, nor drunkards, nor revilers, nor extortioners, shall inherit the kingdom of God" (I Cor. 6:9-10). And also, "Be not deceived: Evil companionships corrupt good morals" (I Cor. 15:33).

Probably the most personal form in which the warning is expressed is that against self-deception. John testified, "If we say that we have no sin, we deceive ourselves, and the truth is not in us" (I John 1:8). Paul urges, "Let no man deceive himself. If any man thinketh that he is wise among you in this world, let him become a fool, that he may become wise" (I Cor. 3:18). James admonished, "But be ye doers of the word, and not hearers only, deluding [or deceiving] your own selves" (Jas. 1:22). He also proclaimed, "If any man thinketh himself to be religious, while he bridleth not his tongue but deceiveth his heart, this man's religion is vain" (Jas. 1:26).

Surely this array of teaching will impress upon everyone who is sincere in his religious conviction the danger of being deceived. It should also cause us to recognize the fact that all of us are probably ignorant on some points as a result of our having been deceived. Or are many of us so deceived that we will pass this matter up by insisting that we are not deceived? Are we going to continue to apply this principle of deception in condemning those who are members of other religious bodies or those individuals within our church group whose ideas are in opposition to ours, but consider ourselves exceptions to the rule and thus refuse or neglect to make personal application of this teaching? There are too many people who have succeeded so well in deceiving themselves that they resemble the case of the patient in the hospital for the mentally ill who declared that he was sane but that everyone else was insane.

Having been made aware of the danger, the prevalence, and the insidiousness of deception, and also of the important part which it has played in our religious beliefs and activities, the next question that engages our attention is, "How have these things come to be?" Why have so many people been deceived?

Everyone knows that the uninformed person in any field is more easily deceived than one who has information. One who does not know clothing material may be sold a cotton suit for one that is made of wool. A person not acquainted with stones may be sold cut glass for a diamond. One who is not versed in the field of investments may be sold worthless paper at an exceedingly high price. And so it is with other things. Offer a small child his choice between a soiled, crumpled, ragged ten dollar bill and a bright, shiny new penny and he will always take the latter for the simple reason that he is ignorant of the values involved. Thus to him the new penny with its bright color, circular form, and metallic quality for rattling appears to be much the better.

Have you ever stopped to consider how we have come into possession of our respective religious ideas? In the majority of cases, were they not given to us in childhood; or did we not accept them at the time when we were not qualified to evaluate them? Did we not accept our ideas in religion in the same way that we have accepted certain ideas in other fields, such as politics, morals, and even many of our evaluations of both people and things? In the same way the religious ideas held by a parent or a friend are passed on to the children. If they are ideas upon what are called doctrinal points in religion, they have determined largely the church group in which the child would be interested and also his attitude toward other such groups. If the idea concerned some act of Christian behavior which has not been classed doctrinal, it served to propagate those individual differences upon Bible questions which we find among members of the respective church groups as well as among religious people generally.

Someone might be disposed to ask "Even though people have come into possession of most of their religious ideas either in childhood or at the time when they were not sufficiently informed to make proper evaluation, why do they not correct their evaluations of religious ideas just as the child corrects his error in monetary values? It is true that the child learns the differences in money values. He learns that he can buy one piece of candy for a penny, but loads of candy for a ten dollar bill, or that he can exchange his ten dollar bill for one thousand pennies. He learns this through meeting objective situations where there are definite, universally accepted standards by which to measure. Unfortunately, in the field of religion this is not the case. Almost regardless of what ideas, or what set of ideas we accept and follow religiously, life's experiences never confront us with an unquestionable evaluation of them. We may find that they are accepted with praise by some but rejected and repudiated by others. Probably unfortunately for us, our relatives and friends, those in whom we are more inclined to place confidence, sanction our ideas as being correct. This especially applies to certain systems of thought. For the endorsement of some of our individual ideas, we must select certain individuals among these friends. Since, however, they do not always agree among themselves, we can always find someone who will agree with us.

In religious teaching, as is true in all other fields in which we are uninformed, the completeness with which we accept the teaching is directly in proportion to the confidence which we have in the teacher. It is evident that this practice of accepting man as authority, especially preachers, has been responsible, and is still responsible, for the multiplicity of conflicting religious ideas that are held and practiced today. Our preachers and church leaders are our authorities today instead of our Bible.

This is just another way of saying that when a religious question arises, instead of our using the intelligence which God has given unto us in the study of his Word, to learn for ourselves what he would have us to do and how he would have us to do it we take our question to some man, generally a preacher, in whom we have placed our confidence. Now this statement is not a charge against any particular church group or denomination, but is merely a statement of fact. It applies to the majority of people in every church group. They are all made up of human beings and this is a common human practice. You will please pardon my illustrating this point by recounting a personal experience. Some years ago I was visiting in the home of an elder of a certain congregation. He is a fine man, held in high esteem by his neighbors, spoken of as a man who has studied the Bible. Upon being seated, he asked me the direct question, "Do you think it is right for a Christian to take part in carnal warfare?" I delayed my answer just a moment so he continued. He said, "Brother 'So and So' believes it is right," naming a preacher. "He said that if he were young he would be willing to take a gun and go to the front himself." Then my host declared that he also believed that it was right. He made no further inquiry about my judgment or understanding in the matter. This man was engaging in one of the most dangerous practices in which a Christian can be engaged, that of quoting a human being as an authority in religious matters. Why do we indulge in such a practice? Why do we not rather go to God's Word, spend a few hours, a few days, a few weeks, or even a few months to learn the answer for ourselves? But it is easier to take what someone else says about it, and since this is what we have always done, it is what we continue to do—accept our religious teaching upon human authority.

We do not say that men are authorities. In fact,

theoretically, we would deny it, but how many times in the last few years has the question of a Christian's participation in carnal warfare been asked? And how many times has it been answered by quoting some man, especially some preacher? Why not study the Bible more? Why not quote it as our authority instead of quoting some preacher? When a person quotes a preacher, a commentary or any other human source in support of a religious idea, it generally indicates one of three things: he has become accustomed to resorting to human authority to support the Bible; he is ignorant of the Bible on that question; or he is attempting to answer a question on which the Bible is not clear. All are dangerous practices. There is no desire whatever to destroy confidence in preachers, that confidence which they deserve and which they have a right to expect; but when we come to the place where we quote them as authority, our confidence has become blind, foolhardiness. That is probably the major factor in the production of our conflicting religious ideas and practices, both denominational and otherwise. So strong is our adherence to this practice that even though men of equal intelligence, of equal education, of equal study, of equal maturity, even within the same church group, contend for ideas which are diametrically opposed to each other, even this is not enough to arouse us from our lethargy or indifference.

It seems that we are prone to forget that preachers are human beings and are heirs of the same general human weaknesses found in other people. We forget

that many of the preachers, if not all of them, have,
like those who are not preachers, accepted many of
the ideas which they preach from other preachers
because of their confidence in them. Not only is this
the case but sometimes these ideas are passed on, seem-
ingly without very careful examination. May I illustrate this by a case which came under my observation
a few years ago. A certain very well-known preacher
made a statement in a radio broadcast in one of the
western states about Jesus' method of teaching. The
statement was not his, neither was it a quotation; but
the use made of it showed that he had accepted the
idea and was willing to pass it on to his hearers. This
statement was not only made on the radio but also
appeared in the press. It was this: "Jesus did not use
enough reasoning in his teaching to make one good
syllogism." A syllogism is a particular form of reasoning in which a major premise or fact is stated, and a
minor premise or fact, followed by a conclusion. An
examination of Jesus' method of teaching shows not
only that he used enough reasoning for many syllogisms
but he actually used syllogistic reasoning. "And he
said unto them, What man shall there be of you, that
shall have one sheep, and if this fall into a pit on the
sabbath day, will he not lay hold on it, and lift it out?
How much then is a man of more value than a sheep!
Wherefore it is lawful to do good on the sabbath day"
(Matt. 12:11-12). "But when the Pharisees heard it,
they said, This man doth not cast out demons, but by
Beelzebub the prince of the demons. And knowing

their thoughts he said unto them, Every kingdom divided against itself is brought to desolation; and every city or house divided against itself shall not stand: and if Satan casteth out Satan, he is divided against himself; how then shall his kingdom stand?" (Matt. 12:24-26). "But the Lord answered him, and said, Ye hypocrites, doth not each one of you on the sabbath loose his ox or his ass from the stall, and lead him away to watering? And ought not this woman, being a daughter of Abraham, whom Satan had bound, lo, these eighteen years, to have been loosed from this bond on the day of the sabbath?" (Luke 13:15-16). Evidently this preacher had not evaluated his statement by the Bible.

Do not forget for a moment that there is no preacher who is infallible. Give careful consideration to Bible teaching from any respectable man, preacher or not, especially if his idea conflicts with yours. Then study the Bible for yourself. Rethink and recheck the ideas which you have held even for many years. Do not get the mistaken idea that you are honoring God by following the teaching of some preacher or some group of preachers. We give God the honor when we use his Book only as the source of our instruction. We show our faith in him by our diligence in the study of his teaching and by our adoption of the New Testament as our manual in daily living.

Are you willing to re-examine those religious ideas which you have accepted in ignorance? Is not the matter sufficiently important to deserve that sort of attention? Do not the multitudinous conflicts which pervade the religious thought suggest the wisdom of studying? It is a personal matter which concerns each one of us. What are we going to do about it?

QUESTIONS ON LECTURE IV

1. What is the main door through which sin has made its entrance into human practices?
2. What is probably one of the greatest evidences of the danger in deception?
3. State the different expressions used in the New Testament to warn against deception.
4. How does a man's religion become vain?
5. What is probably our most common and most dangerous practice relative to the principle of deception?
6. What type of person, or under what condition, is one most easily deceived?
7. Under what conditions have most people come into possession of their religious ideas?
8. Why have our religious deceptions not been corrected as was the child's deception about the ten dollar bill?
9. What practice has been responsible for the great multiplicity of conflicting religious ideas today?
10. Where do we seek for the answers of the most of our religious questions?
11. What is one of the most dangerous practices in which a Christian can engage?
12. When one quotes any human source in support of a religious idea, what does it indicate?
13. We continue in our indifference toward this matter despite what radical conditions?
14. What do we seem to forget about preachers?
15. What evidence is given that they are sometime careless in passing on ideas?
16. What mistaken idea of honoring God is warned against?

LECTURE V

WHY ARE PEOPLE WILLING TO
CONTINUE IN DECEPTION?

IN our examination of the question, "Why Do People Not See the Bible Alike?" which includes differences in individual interpretations as well as differences in interpretations by church groups, we have found the basic cause to be ignorance. We have found ignorance to be due to lack of study and the ease with which people can be deceived. We have found that people have been easily deceived in the field of religious ideas, because of the fact that religious teachings have been accepted by most people at the time when they lacked information necessary for arriving at an intelligent decision. Hence, they were accepted because of confidence in the teacher without evaluating them upon Bible authority. We have also found that one of the reasons for people remaining deceived is that life's experiences have not provided objective measures for the ideas that are being held. Beginning at this point, we shall consider another reason why people have been easily deceived and why they have been willing to continue in the deception.

This other cause is a kindred human weakness, being a product of little learning and of self-deceit. It likewise becomes one of the major influences in self-deceit, thus completing the vicious circle and chaining one

like a bond servant to his own ideas. It is conceit.
From the New Testament, our source book, we present
the following statements which not only show the
recognition of this human weakness, but give some
description of it, warning against it, and admonition
to dethrone it. "For if a man thinketh himself to be
something when he is nothing, he deceiveth himself"
(Gal. 6:3). "For I say, through the grace that was given
me, to every man that is among you, not to think of
himself more highly than he ought to think; but so to
think as to think soberly, according as God hath dealt
to each man a measure of faith" (Rom. 12:3). "Be of
the same mind one toward another. Set not your mind
on high things, but condescend to things that are lowly.
Be not wise in your own conceits" (Rom. 12:16). "For
I would not, brethren, have you ignorant of this
mystery, lest ye be wise in your own conceits, that a
hardening in part hath befallen Israel, until the fulness
of the Gentiles be come in" (Rom. 11:25). "Because
that, knowing God, they glorified him not as God,
neither gave thanks; but became vain in their reasonings, and their senseless heart was darkened. Profess-
ing themselves to be wise, they become fools" (Rom.
1:21-22). This last statement shows how deceit distorts
one's sense of values. He thinks himself to be wise.
God knows him to be a fool. "Let no man deceive
himself. If any man thinketh that he is wise among
you in this world, let him become a fool, that he may
become wise" (I Cor. 3:18). Here Paul would instruct
the conceited man that before he can become wise, he

must become a fool. This is another way of saying that the first step toward learning is a recognition of one's own ignorance. Paul continues with a statement that should warn us not to become too engrossed in our own wisdom, "For the wisdom of this world is foolishness with God. For it is written, He that taketh the wise in their craftiness: and again, The Lord knoweth the reasonings of the wise, that they are vain" (I Cor. 3:19-20). Another statement to the same people, "Wherefore let him that thinketh he standeth take heed lest he fall" (I Cor. 10:12). This may not only be heard as the warning of divine wisdom but the voice of experience as well. Paul had been wise in his own conceit, living in all good conscience, blaspheming and persecuting to learn later the exceeding sinfulness of his practices.

It is shocking when we realize how completely one is able to deceive himself in regard to his own state or condition. This had happened with the church at Laodicea. John draws the picture in these words, "Because thou sayest, I am rich, and have gotten riches, and have need of nothing; and knowest not that thou art the wretched one and miserable and poor and blind and naked" (Rev. 3:17). The people thought themselves rich and in need of nothing when in reality they were "miserable and poor and blind and naked." Jesus also shows us how completely blinded men may become because of their conceit, how perfectly satisfied they may be with their manner of life. They may even have the confidence to plead their case at the judgment bar of God on those practices which they have so confidently followed here. He said, "Many will say to me in that day, Lord, Lord, did we not prophesy by thy name, and by thy name cast out demons, and by thy name do many mighty works? And then will I profess unto them, I never knew you: depart from me, ye that work iniquity" (Matt. 7:22-23). Surely this descriptive statement of what can be the result of that complacency which accompanies man's self-conceit should warn each one of us in such form as would awaken us from our lethargy to study God's Word as we have never studied it before. We should consider man's weaknesses and try in every way to see that we have removed every hindrance to understanding God's will, for Jesus says, "Not every one that saith unto me, Lord, Lord, shall enter into the kingdom of heaven, but he that doeth the will of my Father who is in heaven" (Matt. 7:21).

This tendency toward implicit self-confidence is only a modified form of the childish trait which we have beheld over and over again. It is illustrated by the child who has first learned that he can make a hissing sound by blowing air through his teeth, when he calls out, "Watch me whistle! I can whistle!" It is also illustrated by the reactions of the child who is being shown how to do some particular piece of work in which he is interested. Often before half of the instruction is given, he begins to jump up and down and urgently insist, "I know, I know. Let me do it." Sometimes he can, but many times he cannot.

This same element of human nature is present in

older people.   In most cases it is less conspicuous, as the impulsiveness of youth has become subdued by the experiences of age.   The small number of people with whom this has not been the case have been described by some of their fellows as being conceited.   However, this feeling of self-confidence is a part of us all, though it may vary somewhat in degree.   There is also wide variation in circumstances and conditions which will arouse it to the point of self-assertion.   Within itself, it is not bad.   On the contrary, it is absolutely necessary to man's accomplishment.   But like all other good things, it must be guarded and controlled; otherwise it may come to be used detrimentally.   The danger point in self-confidence has been reached when it goes beyond or pushes one beyond what is fully justified by his information or skill.   This is markedly illustrated by the readiness with which people who have not experienced responsibility of rearing children, especially bachelors, spinsters, and young preachers, boldly set forth the procedures which should be followed, and unhesitatingly declare what they would do under such and such conditions.   And have not all of us felt and talked the same way?   But how many who have had children of their own still feel their self-sufficiency?

We find illustrations of this same human weakness in our New Testament record.   A scribe came to our Saviour on one occasion and said confidently, "Teacher, I will follow thee whithersoever thou goest" (Matt. 8:19).   Jesus knew that he had spoken where his information did not justify, so he gently rebuked him by saying, "The foxes have holes, and the birds of the heaven have nests; but the Son of man hath not where to lay his head" (Matt. 8:20). Jesus told the disciples that all would be offended in him, "But Peter answered and said unto him, If all shall be offended in thee, I will never be offended. Jesus said unto him, Verily I say unto thee, that this night, before the cock crow, thou shalt deny me thrice. Peter saith unto him, Even if I must die with thee, yet will I not deny thee. Likewise also said all the disciples" (Matt. 26:33-35). Here we see conceit at a most dangerous pitch. It has taken possession of Peter to such an extent that it causes him to place his own ignorance above the knowledge of his Master, the one whom he has confessed to be the Son of the living God. Since Peter, who had been associated with his Lord for some three and one-half years, could become so blinded, should not we be constrained to consider the warning that the same dangerous element of human nature is deeply embedded in each one of us?

When the mother of James and John made request of Jesus that one of her sons should sit on his right hand and one on his left in his kingdom, Jesus reminded her that their aspirations were forcing them beyond their knowledge when he answered, "Ye know not what ye ask" (Matt. 20:22). He further emphasized this point by the question, "Are ye able to drink the cup that I am about to drink?" (Matt. 20:22). But James and John were so blinded by human desire that they failed to completely get Jesus' lesson. Led on by their conceit, they further supported their petition by their answer, "We are able." Here we have a double expression of their self-confidence or conceit. The request for the places of honor in Jesus' kingdom indicates that James and John were confident that they understood the nature of the kingdom and were certain that the positions for which they asked would be included in his organization. The record shows that they had completely misunderstood the nature of Jesus' kingdom and that this request had grown out of their ignorance. Their answer, "We are able," shows how this human element led them on to accept the responsibility of which they had no definite information. I sometimes wonder if our understanding of Jesus' kingdom today is not similar to that of James and John at this time, a misunderstanding. And I wonder if some of the places of honor which we have set about preparing for ourselves are not as much out of harmony with its operation as those requested by James and John.

Other expressions are used in the New Testament to refer to the same human weakness. The descriptive phrase, "puffed up," is repeatedly used by the apostle Paul. In one short statement of contrast the apostle shows us the source of our trouble. "Knowledge puffeth up, but love edifieth" (I Cor. 8:1). That is, knowledge puffeth up, giving that false feeling of greatness, but love edifieth, buildeth up, and gives the person real greatness through humility. The person whose heart is filled with love for God and man is forgetful of himself, his thoughts being pervaded and controlled by his sincere purpose to honor God by serving man. If, however, he is lacking in love for God and man, his thoughts turn to himself; he becomes puffed up and he is lacking in real understanding. Thus the apostle says, "If any man thinketh that he knoweth anything, he knoweth not yet as he ought to know" (I Cor. 8:2).

In writing to the young man Timothy, the apostle gives him a picture of the man that is puffed up. "If any man teacheth a different doctrine, and consenteth not to sound words, even the words of our Lord Jesus Christ, and to the doctrine which is according to godliness; he is puffed up, knowing nothing, but doting about questionings and disputes of words, whereof cometh envy, strife, railings, evil surmisings, wranglings of men corrupted in mind and bereft of the truth, supposing that godliness is a way of gain" (I Tim. 6:3-5). He also names this with many other selfish traits in his description of the evil men in the last days. "But know this, that in the last days grievous times shall come. For men shall be lovers of self, lovers of money, boastful, haughty, railers, disobedient to parents, unthankful, unholy, without natural affection, implacable, slanderers, without self-control, fierce, no lovers of good, traitors, headstrong, puffed up, lovers of pleasure rather than lovers of God; holding a form of godliness, but having denied the power thereof: from these also turn away" (II Tim. 3:1-5).

Since these two statements from the apostle Paul show the evil results of being puffed up and other wicked practices which accompany it, we should not make the mistake of allowing ourselves to be led to think that only the man with the wicked heart may become puffed up. On the contrary, Paul shows us that a person may have many excellent characteristics and Christian qualities and still be in danger of falling under this blighting influence. In describing the qualifications of a bishop, Paul says, "Must be without reproach, the husband of one wife, temperate, soberminded, orderly, given to hospitality, apt to teach; no brawler, no striker; but gentle, not contentious, no lover of money; one that ruleth well his own house, having his children in subjection with all gravity; (but if a man knoweth not how to rule his own house, how shall he take care of the church of God?) not a novice, lest being puffed up he fall into the condemnation of the devil" (I Tim. 3:2-6). This being the case, no man should consider himself the exception, but should constantly guard himself against this human weakness, striving to attain and maintain the attitude set forth by the apostle Paul in these words, "In love of the brethren be tenderly affectioned one to another; in honor preferring one another" (Rom. 12:10).

Thus far we have considered largely the detailed warning which has come to us through the apostle Paul. Let us now turn to the personal teachings of the Master himself with a prayer that we may not only become more conscious of the lurking danger in self-conceit, but that we may drink of his spirit and partake of his likeness.

In the record of Jesus' life and teaching, no use is

made of the word conceit, nor of the phrase, "puffed up." However, his teaching, both by example and precept, makes it unmistakably clear that human conceit is in direct opposition to it all, that the feeling of self-sufficiency is not only a handicap to Christian living, but a stumbling block to the acceptance of Christian teaching. Jesus shows the antagonism between this element of human nature and one of the basic traits of Christian character by the use of contrasting terms, exalted and humble. When Jesus beheld how the guests at the marriage feasts chose out the chief seats, he warned them of the danger of such a practice, and of the humiliation that they might suffer upon the arrival of a more honorable guest. Then after showing the self-seeking guests how they might obtain more glory by taking a lower seat, he declared unto them the eternal principle, "For every one that exalteth himself shall be humbled; and he that humbleth himself shall be exalted" (Luke 14:11). On another occasion Jesus illustrates the contrasting effects of these two attitudes in the act of worship. "And he spake also this parable unto certain who trusted in themselves that they were righteous, and set all others at nought: Two men went up into the temple to pray; the one a Pharisee, and the other a publican. The Pharisee stood and prayed thus with himself, God, I thank thee, that I am not as the rest of men, extortioners, unjust, adulterers, or even as this publican. I fast twice in the week; I give tithes of all that I get. But the publican, standing afar off, would not lift up so much as his eyes unto heaven, but smote his breast, saying, God, be thou merciful to me a sinner. I say unto you, This man went down to his house justified rather than the other: for every one that exalteth himself shall be humbled; but he that humbleth himself shall be exalted" (Luke 18: 9-14).

Speaking to the multitudes and to his disciples regarding the scribes and Pharisees, Jesus described some of their religious practices which resulted from this self-conceited attitude. Do we have any of these effects today? "Yea, they bind heavy burdens and grievous to be borne, and lay them on men's shoulders; but they themselves will not move them with their finger. But all their works they do to be seen of men: for they make broad their phylacteries, and enlarge the borders of their garments, and love the chief place at feasts, and the chief seats in the synagogues, and the salutations in the marketplaces, and to be called of men, Rabbi. But be not ye called Rabbi: for one is your teacher, and all ye are brethren. And call no man your father on the earth: for one is your Father, even he who is in heaven. Neither be ye called masters: for one is your master, even the Christ. But he that is greatest among you shall be your servant. And whosoever shall exalt himself shall be humbled; and whosoever shall humble himself shall be exalted" (Matt. 23:4-12).

The disciples themselves during the time of Jesus' personal ministry were not free from this same weakness. The question arose time and time again, "Who is the greatest in the kingdom of heaven?" It was in answer to this question that Jesus used a little child as an object lesson. "And he called to him a little child, and set him in the midst of them, and said, Verily I say unto you, Except ye turn, and become as little children, ye shall in no wise enter into the kingdom of heaven. Whosoever therefore shall humble himself as this little child, the same is the greatest in the kingdom of heaven" (Matt. 18:2-4). Here Jesus was telling his disciples, and he is still telling us, that man must forget his own wisdom and power, abandon his own feeling of superiority, recognize that it is not within man that walketh to direct his steps, that he may feel his dependence as he did in the early days of childhood; that he may look to his heavenly father with that same implicit trust that he placed in his mother in those days gone by before he had learned to doubt. Then mother's word was the criterion by which all things were measured. Any failure in agreement was the sure signal for discredit and discard. God grant that we may learn to cling to his sacred teaching with the same purity and simplicity.

QUESTIONS ON LECTURE V

1. What human weakness is a product of a little learning and self-deceit?
2. Give some warnings against conceit.
3. What must the conceited man do before he can become wise?
4. What character have we especially studied who was wise in his own conceit?

5. Give evidences of the completeness with which man is able to deceive himself.
6. Where did this tendency toward implicit self-confidence begin?
7. Show that it is not necessarily something bad, but a bad use of something good.
8. Give a number of New Testament illustrations of this human weakness.
9. What expression does Paul use repeatedly in speaking of this condition?
10. In what particular connection does Paul use it that suggests that it might happen to the best of us?
11. What terms did Jesus use to set forth the same idea?
12. Give some of his lessons to this effect.
13. What practices that indicate this conceit did Jesus warn his disciples against?
14. What special object lesson on humility did Jesus give his disciples that we should never forget?

HUMAN CONCEIT AND HUMAN ACTION

WE continue our discussion of "Why Do People Not See the Bible Alike?" but it is hoped that the repetition of this question will not cause you to think that the sole purpose of this study is to answer it. We do want to answer the question fully and satisfactorily, but we hope and pray that we may accomplish something that is far more important. Our real purpose, and may God grant you that attitude of heart and mind so vital to its accomplishment, is to present such an analysis of human weaknesses that you will be made aware of your own greatest personal danger. It is clear, from the materials that have been presented, that its deepest roots are to be found in your ignorance of God's Word. It is fine to have a zeal for God, but it is pitiable for one to have zeal without knowledge. This led many of the Jews to destruction.

It would do the same for you or me. We have seen that deceit is a universal human weakness that not only flourishes where ignorance is, but frequently serves to increase our ignorance as well as become the agent through which ignorance blinds us and holds us to our old errors. We have also been reminded of the fact that we accepted many of our religious ideas in childhood or at a time when we were not capable of judging them by the Word of God. Furthermore, it was evident from the last study that conceit (that unjustifiable feeling of self-confidence and self-satisfaction which many times pervades and controls our actions without our being aware of its presence) is largely responsible for the rejection of Christianity and also for the failure of many who have accepted Christianity to follow its teaching. Our study of conceit thus far has been concerned with precepts and principles bearing directly upon the subject, but we shall never fully understand the part that conceit plays in our religious life until we realize how closely it is interlinked with our actions.

If you have come to think of yourself more highly than you ought to think, exalting yourself, becoming puffed up, then your own self-conceit has come between you and the sun of righteousness thus casting its eerie shadows across your soul, blinding your intelligence, distorting your thinking, deforming your perspective, unbalancing your sense of values, and misdirecting your efforts. And thus the things of earth are caused to glow with a false light that lures you on into the forgetfulness of self-satisfaction.

We should remember with Paul that though, "I know nothing against myself; yet am I not hereby justified" (I Cor. 4:4). "For not he that commendeth himself is approved, but whom the Lord commendeth" (II Cor. 10:18). Also, "And he hath said unto me, My grace is sufficient for thee: for my power is made perfect in weakness. Most gladly therefore will I rather glory in my weaknesses, that the power of Christ may rest upon me. Wherefore I take pleasure in weaknesses, in injuries, in necessities, in persecutions, in distresses, for Christ's sake: for when I am weak, then am I strong" (II Cor. 12:9-10). When we feel our weakness, we recognize our insufficiency, our dependence upon God, our need for his power and wisdom; then are we strong. The converse is also true. When we feel self-sufficient and independent, confident of our ability, satisfied with our knowledge and content with our accomplishments, when we are strong in our own sight, then are we weak.

Of this effect of one's thought of himself upon his daily living, Jesus gives us no analytical discussion. Neither does he make direct denunciation of conceit in those scathing terms which man's narrow human way of thinking might lead him to expect. In fact, Jesus does not even use the Greek word that is translated conceit. However, his statement of the requirements of discipleship shows that one's self is the only real obstacle to Christian obedience, that you are your own greatest hindrance to eternal happiness and that your real stone of stumbling is your attitude toward yourself. As is true of his other teaching, his instruction is clearly and concisely stated. In this his style is in conformity with his purpose, to teach those who are willing to hear, to tell those who want to know.

Despite the simplicity and straightforward character of his declaration, it has been misinterpreted and misapplied by many. For this reason, it is thought advisable, for the sake of clarity and emphasis, to make a very careful examination of it. "Then said Jesus unto his disciples, If any man would come after me, let him deny himself, and take up his cross, and follow me" (Matt. 16:24). Here Jesus states three things that are necessary to every man who would be his disciple: "Deny himself, take up his cross, follow me." The universality of these requirements is evidenced in his introductory phrase, "If any man" which includes all races—white, black, red, yellow, or brown—in all ages. The first requisite for discipleship for everyone is to deny himself.

Just what did Jesus mean by this expression? In common usage the expression "deny self" is always followed by the name of the thing denied. For example, we say, "The boy denied himself an education that he might support the family." "The girl denied herself a summer vacation that she might buy a new dress." "The mother denied herself comforts at home that she might send her boy to college." "Livingstone denied himself the comforts of civilization that he might do missionary work in Africa." We have followed this practice so universally that should we speak of someone denying himself and fail to name or clearly imply the thing which he has denied himself, the question, "What did he deny himself?" would be immediately forthcoming. But this is not the way that Jesus used the expression. Jesus said, "If anyone would come after me, let him deny himself." Not "let him deny to himself, this or that," but "himself" is the direct object of deny. What did Jesus mean? Can we break away

from our use of this expression sufficiently to understand the full meaning of his?

Let us begin our search for his meaning by an examination of the context. The setting or conditions under
which the statement is made, like the background of
a picture, provides perspective which often aids im-
measureably the proper understanding of the idea.
After having taught the disciples on many occasions
and having led them to believe that he was the Messiah,
and having heard this faith expressed through Peter's
confession "Thou art the Christ, the son of the Living
God," Jesus began to make known unto them that
which he had formerly uttered only in dark sayings.
He declared, "That he would go to Jerusalem, suffer
many things of the elders, chief priests and scribes and
be killed, and the third day be raised up." The idea
was so new, so shocking, so different from that which
was expected by the disciples, that Peter rebuked his
Lord, saying, "Be it far from thee, Lord: this shall
never be unto thee" (Matt. 16:22). Whereupon, Jesus
said unto Peter, "Get thee behind me, Satan: thou art
a stumbling block unto me: for thou mindest not the
things of God, but the things of men" (Matt. 16:23).
What is the gist of this conversation? Jesus told Peter
and the other apostles that he was to be crucified.
Peter rejected the teaching, saying "This shall never
be." Whereupon, Jesus addressed Peter as Satan and
told him that his refusal of this teaching which came
from God, by following his own ideas, the things of
men, he would make himself a stumbling block unto

Jesus, who was pledged to submit himself completely unto God's teaching, including the crucifixion. And immediately after showing Peter what he had done, the record states "Then said Jesus unto his disciples, If any man would come after me, let him deny himself."

May we recall just here how Jesus had repeatedly told the disciples that he came not to do his will but the will of the Father, that the teaching was not his but the teaching of the Father. By the close connection of this lesson with the preceding conversation, it is evident that it is an outgrowth of the conversation and expresses an idea very similar in nature. May we turn to this conversation once again, hearing its content from Jesus' personal viewpoint. Jesus has just told the disciples that he is going to Jerusalem and submit himself unreservedly to God's teaching in regard to the crucifixion, as he had to all of God's teaching in the past. Thus he reserved to himself no right of decision, no will of his own. His ideas, his feeling, his wishes, whatever they might be, were never to be the controlling factor in his behavior. He had denied himself completely, even when confronted with the sufferings and anguish of the cross, saying "not my will but thine be done." When Peter refused to accept this idea as it applied to his master, Jesus then applied it to his disciples, that if anyone would be his disciple, he must likewise deny himself, give up all rights to his ideas, his wishes, his feelings, recognize his littleness and insufficiency, turn away from his own wisdom. "If anyone would be my disciple, let him deny himself."

It is a well-known fact that our Bible was not originally written in English, but that it is a translated book. Hence, the expression "deny self" is a translation from the Greek language. Since it happens that this expression has been considerably abused in its usage, suppose we look for a moment at other translations of the word Jesus spoke. Probably they will bring his idea to us with greater clarity.

The word which is here translated "deny" has also been translated "disregard." By putting this translation into our text, we have, "If any man would be my disciple, let him disregard himself." Is not this what Jesus did? Another translation which has been used is "lose sight of." Read this into our text and it says, "If anyone would be my disciple, let him lose sight of himself." We shall notice one other translation. Due to the importance which we have attached to ownership or possession, it is probably the strongest of the three, "totally disown." Reading it into our text, we have, "If anyone would be my disciple, let him totally disown himself." How true was this of our Saviour and how necessary it is of us.

In this lesson, as in all other study of God's Word, we should not be content until we have studied the matter from every angle. There is one other source which we may check. Jesus taught his twelve disciples, and they have passed his teaching on to their fellows. Is Jesus' teaching that has come to us through them in perfect agreement with the idea of self-denial as presented here?

We turn first to the record of James where we find this admonition, "Wherefore putting away all filthiness and overflowing of wickedness, receive with meekness the implanted word, which is able to save your souls" (Jas. 1:21). What does James tell us to put away? "All filthiness and overflowing of wickedness." From whence does this come? Is it not the result of man's following his own ideas, his own wishes, his own lusts in the matter? Is not James admonishing them to deny self, to turn away from their own way, and receive with meekness the implanted word which is able to save their souls?

Peter gives the admonition in these words, "Putting away therefore all wickedness, and all guile, and hypocrisies, and envies, and all evil speakings, as newborn babes, long for spiritual milk which is without guile, that ye may grow thereby unto salvation" (I Pet. 2: 1-2). We find the same twofold admonition, "put away," and "long for." What is the source of wickedness, guile, hypocrisy, envy, and evil speaking? Are they not the results of man's efforts to direct his own steps? Do they not indicate that man has not come to disregard himself, to lose sight of himself, or to totally disown himself? Or may we ask, would these practices ever result from following the teachings of him who died that we might live?

The apostle Paul, who tells us that he received his teaching from above, writes, "That ye put away, as concerning your former manner of life, the old man, that waxeth corrupt after the lusts of deceit; and that ye be renewed in the spirit of your mind, and put on the new man, that after God hath been created in righteousness and holiness of truth" (Eph. 4:22-24). Also, "Lie not one to another; seeing that ye have put off the old man with his doings, and have put on the new man, that is being renewed unto knowledge after the image of him that created him" (Col. 3:9-10). Thus the admonition to put off the old man that waxeth corrupt after the lust of deceit or by following one's own lusts or desires must be done before the new man can be put on. In his appeal to the Corinthian people to abstain from fornication, Paul reasoned with them thus, "Or know ye not that your body is a temple of the Holy Spirit which is in you, which ye have from God? and ye are not your own; for ye were bought with a price: glorify God therefore in your body" (I Cor. 6:19-20). Here is a statement of their relationship to God, "Ye are not your own, for ye were bought with a price." This Paul offers as the reason why they should cease following their own lusts. Such practices were plainly in violation of their relationship. The right of ownership or possession certainly carries the right of direction. They should no longer be following their own way but the teachings of their Master. They have accepted the purchase price. They have become Christians. They have entered into this relationship which requires that they dethrone themselves, that they surrender once and for all the right of directing their own steps. Ownership, which is used here as a figure of speech, certainly implies the right to tell a person

what to do and also how to do it. Is not this just what
Jesus was saying in his statement, "If anyone would
come after me, let him deny [disregard, lose sight of,
totally disown] himself"? Did not Jesus show the ab-
surdity of such an inconsistency when he asked, "And
why call ye me, Lord, Lord, and do not the things
which I say" (Luke 6:46)?

In speaking of this principle formerly, it has been
referred to as a requirement of discipleship. It is highly
probable that this expression does not convey exactly
the right idea. Such expressions as "conditions of
salvation," and "requirements of discipleship," have
taken on an unnatural rigidity due to the wide usage
of such expressions. From the usage of these and
other kindred expressions many people have come to
think of Jehovah as an all-powerful God and the plan
which he has provided for man's salvation as an arbi-
trary set of demands or requirements selected or
determined solely by their peculiar power for pleasing
the divine being without any consideration for man's
nature and needs. It is very apparent that this is not
the case. We should not only remember that our God
is a God of power, but also a God of mercy, of knowledge and of wisdom.

Reasoning from these facts, one should expect God's
teachings to be adjusted to man's needs and nature.
This is just the case in this teaching on self-denial.
Until one has dethroned his own wisdom, he cannot
accept that wisdom which is from above. Until one has
exchanged his conceit for humility, he will not follow

the instruction of another. Until he repudiates his own thoughts and accepts those of the Almighty, he will never be able to walk in his way. "My thoughts are not your thoughts, neither are your ways my ways, saith Jehovah. For as the heavens are higher than the earth, so are my ways higher than your ways, and my thoughts than your thoughts" (Isa. 55:8-9).

Consider this simple illustration. Mrs. Jones makes a visit to a friend in a neighboring town. At dinner she is served a piece of most delicious pie, the like of which she has never before tasted. Conforming to the regular practice of women who prepare their own meals, when Mrs. Jones has eaten a few bites, talked about how good the pie is, inquired of her hostess where she learned to make such desserts, she asks if she may have a copy of the receipt. Her hostess very graciously promises to provide her with a copy before she leaves for home. When her visit is over, Mrs. Jones returns home with an exact copy of the receipt by which the wonderful pie was made. A few weeks later Mrs. Jones expects special company. She decides that she will try the new receipt. She goes into the kitchen, reads over her receipt, opens up her cabinet, checks to see that she has all necessary ingredients, carefully reviews her receipt, and then starts to work. She follows the directions to the letter until she comes to the item of butter. The receipt calls for two tablespoonfuls of butter. Mrs. Jones pauses, rereads, and then she discusses the matter with herself. "That looks like too much butter. I have baked lots of good pies. In fact, I have the reputation of being the best pie-maker in the community. I believe one and one-half tablespoonfuls of butter will be better. So that's what I am going to use." After putting in that amount, she continues with the receipt just as it is until everything else required has been included and mixed in exact keeping with instructions. Then Mrs. Jones decides it would be better if she added a pinch of cinnamon. This she does, puts the pie in the oven, and bakes according to instruction. The pie may turn out to be altogether satisfactory. In fact, she may *think* it is an improvement upon the one she ate in the home of her friend. But did she make the pie described in her receipt? Certainly not. Why? Simply because she thought that she knew better. How different it would have been if Mrs. Jones had been a novice at cooking instead of a cook with a community reputation. She would have put her complete trust in the receipt. As it is, however, Mrs. Jones is puffed up by her own knowledge. She is conceited. And so are we all. We put confidence in our own wisdom and by doing so disrespect the wisdom of our God. This God knows far better than do we. So long as one fails to recognize his own ignorance on any subject, he is not ready to accept the teaching of another. So long as men are blinded by human conceit, just so long they will continue to follow their own ways which in many cases are represented by modifications of God's ways. God knew that human conceit was the source of the greatest antagonism toward his wisdom and thus he teaches us, through his Son, that if any man would be his disciple, he must deny himself.

QUESTIONS ON LECTURE VI

1. What is the real purpose of this study?
2. What two things are conceit largely responsible for?
3. What are the human effects of conceit?
4. When did Paul say he was strong?
5. What is the real obstacle to Christian obedience?
6. Name the three things necessary to discipleship.
7. In Jesus' statement, what is the direct object of deny?
8. What was Peter doing that caused Jesus to address him as Satan?
9. What had Jesus emphasized in regard to his teaching?
10. Give three other translations of the Greek word that is translated "deny."
11. Give teachings from Peter, James, and Paul that are in harmony with this idea.
12. How did Paul express the Christian relationship to God that implies that man has no right to govern himself?
13. How did Jesus express the same idea?
14. How have some people come to think of Jehovah?
15. What is necessary in order to walk in Jehovah's ways?
16. Why did Mrs. Jones not faithfully follow her receipt?
17. How long will people continue to follow their own ways?

LECTURE VII
MAN'S MOST DANGEROUS PRACTICE

IN our efforts to answer the question, "Why Do People Not See the Bible Alike?" attention has been given to three interrelated factors—ignorance, deceit, and conceit. We have seen that the most pernicious and persistent form of ignorance is the result of deception and conceit, that deception is the natural outcome of ignorance and conceit, and that conceit (unjustified self-confidence) is the fruit of deception and ignorance. This is the most complex vicious circle, the most dangerous combination of influences, the most blighting coalition of human weaknesses to be found in the whole realm of human activity and endeavor. So long as a human being remains the victim of this triumvirate of his own weaknesses, so long will he be fettered like a slave to his own narrow human interpretation of the divine wisdom revealed in the Bible; and so long will continue the multitude of diverse ideas on numerous points in Bible teaching.

Will you and I ever become big enough to recognize our littleness? Will we ever be able to dethrone our weaknesses that blind us to the great things of life and the proper understanding of that wisdom which came down from above? Until we do, there is no hope for seeing the Bible alike; or rather there is no hope for understanding the Bible teaching. The important question is not how much you can tell your neighbor, but how much will you allow God to tell you? This suggests another form for the question with which these discussions began, "Why have so many people come to believe that God has told them so many different things?"

The human factors that are responsible for the existing conditions have already been discussed (ignorance, deceit, and conceit), but our answer would remain incomplete and lose much of its practical value without the consideration of the major human practice through which these factors are developed and in which their blighting effects upon the lives of professed followers of Christ are most destructively wrought. It is the practice of comparing ourselves with others. Paul found it among the Corinthian people and gave us a statement of it in his second epistle. "For we are not bold to number or compare ourselves with certain of them that commend themselves: but they themselves measuring themselves by themselves, and comparing themselves with themselves, are without understanding" (II Cor. 10:12). Here we have three facts stated. First, there were those who commended themselves. Second, they measured themselves by themselves. Third, they were without understanding. Let us consider the statements in the reverse order.

"They were without understanding." This is a very simple statement which contains no harsh or cruel words of condemnation, no description of heinous crimes or acts of dishonor, no warnings against wicked thoughts or vile imaginations; but it is a description of a condition which will permit indulgence in many evil practices and that without any sense of guilt. It is the description of people bereft of their sense of values. They neither know where they are going, nor in what direction. They may call evil good, and good evil, or put darkness for light and light for darkness. They are lost in the desert of their own mistakes. They are enshrouded in their own wisdom. "If therefore the light that is in thee be darkness, how great is the darkness!" (Matt. 6:23). This is about the most hopeless and most helpless state of human existence with respect to any sphere of human endeavor to which it applies. Yes, "they were without understanding." They were acting like people who were without understanding. We learn from the first Corinthian letter about their divisions, their fornication, their lawsuits, their misunderstanding of marriage relationships, their confusion over eating things sacrificed to idols, their desecration of the Supper, their contention about spiritual gifts, and their repudiation of the resurrection. Since similar divisions, contentions and confusions are prevalent today among church people, even within local congregations and among people of unquestionable sincerity, is it not reasonable to believe that the source of much of our trouble is the same as that of the Corinthians—without understanding?

Paul did not leave us to guess at the cause of this direful condition. It was the result of their own practice. They measured themselves by themselves, and compared themselves with themselves. Why did this practice leave them without understanding? Because it took away their standard of measure. Or, to speak more exactly, they had individually replaced the sacred, unchangeable teaching of Almighty God, which was given to them as the standard of righteous living, with the varying, changing, conflicting practices of individuals. Or, to put the matter another way, they had allowed human ideas and practices to distort their understanding of the teaching that they had received, thus providing them with varied and conflicting interpretations; and, being bereft of their understanding, they accepted them for the truth. Without doubt, many of them were fully sincere in the matter. But how could they make such a mistake in a matter that concerned their eternal destiny?

It is true that when we measure their mistake in terms of the consequences, it was an error of great magnitude; but when we measure it in terms of digression from normal acceptable human behavior, it shrinks to virtual insignificance. All of our values are relative and frequently change. We arrive at them through the method of comparison. One object is large or small in comparison with another. Where actual trade or exchange is the occasion of evaluation, we compare with a unit of measure for dimensions but the actual price paid is determined by the quality as compared with that of other similar articles. We pay more for this suit because in some ways it is better than that one (or we think it is better). We have followed this practice all

of our lives.   In fact, we have known no other.   Even in
our estimate of personal qualities, we resort to the same
practice.   Yes, we have always measured ourselves by
others.

When we were small children, we were shorter or
taller than someone else; we could run faster, or not
so fast; we could throw farther or not so far, etc.   The
facts had little personal significance, so were readily
accepted.   As we grew older, our personal interest became a factor.   We were taller than someone else, could
run faster, throw farther, were more handsome, more
intelligent, etc., because we selected the child with
whom to compare, or we selected the quality or skill
with which to compare that would give us the advantage.   We tended to ignore all other children or
qualities as the case might be.   Later we learned that
it was not always best to excel, for more was expected
of us.   When we desired to protect or excuse ourselves,
we compared with someone that was more capable.
If father or mother were assigning a task, we would
state our comparison with brother or sister on some
point that would show that he or she should do the task.
He was larger, or quicker, or knew more about it; or
we did not feel well, or had a sore finger or some other
ground for inferiority.   We had learned to adjust the
practice to the conditions in order to appear the best
or get the best.   We do yet.

Since people have followed this practice of comparison all of their lives in their dealings with each other,
either to show personal advantage or to gain personal

advantage, and since they are more conscious of the presence and judgments of the people about them than they are of God's presence, it is not surprising that Paul found the Corinthians "measuring themselves by themselves." Neither is it surprising that people today, that we, are continuing the same practice, and with the same results. So, as long as the practice continues, so long will our present differences and confusion continue, and so long will we fail to meet the first requisite of a true follower of the Lord Jesus Christ. "If any man would come after me, let him deny himself" (Matt. 16:24). Will we ever come to understand this teaching? Will we ever recognize the fact that man is his only real enemy? Will we ever dethrone self and enthrone Jehovah? Will we ever acquire that humility that will truly exalt God, count others better than oneself (Phil. 2:3), not think more highly of oneself than we ought to think (Rom. 12:3)?

By this practice of measuring themselves by themselves they were not only without understanding, reduced to ignorance, but Paul's first descriptive statement makes it clear that they had deceived themselves and had become conceited. They commended themselves. No man can commend himself in those things that pertain to righteousness without having been deceived. Jesus admonished, "When ye shall have done all the things that are commanded you, say, We are unprofitable servants; we have done that which it was our duty to do" (Luke 17:10). As long as man measures himself by the example of his Lord he will never find occasion for being puffed up, but as long as he selects his own measure among his fellows, under the influence of personal self-seeking, consciously or unconsciously, he will be without understanding, deceived, and conceited.

Here we see the vicious circle in action, driven by the practice of measuring by false standards or making partial, biased comparisons. As is the case with all circles, it is difficult to find the beginning or the end, as there appears to be neither. So whether its point of origin is to be found in deception or in conceit, we may never know, and to end it completely we may never be able; but we should recognize the fact that, since all are human beings, each of us is in danger of falling victim to its power. The majority of people would deny being ignorant, deceived, or conceited in most religious matters, but they would accuse the person of such who does not agree with their ideas. These are cases in which they are deceived in regard to their being deceived.

Thus, we have a vicious circle within the vicious circle. Herein lies the point of greatest danger because it conceals the very existence of danger. There are probably no greater evidences that many people have fallen victims to this blinding condition than the conflicting religious ideas of the present day (both individual and denominational) and the attitude toward them. To recognize that these differences exist is unavoidable. Why have they multiplied instead of being resolved? Was it not because many people were not only deceived, but so completely deceived that they never even considered that they could be deceived? Consequently, did not they assume that they were right, with little or no consideration of the origin of their ideas and conclude that all who did not agree with them were wrong? And thus, have we not assumed the defensive instead of the inquiring attitude? Have we not been more ready to condemn the other person's idea than to examine our own? Will we ever recognize that we are human and are beset by human weaknesses?

The very nature of the case makes it difficult for the one who is ignorant, deceived and conceited to become aware of his condition. If, however, he may be led to discontinue the practice that distorted his standard of measure and took away his understanding, he may regain proper perspective, restore his proper sense of values, and cease to pervert the right way of the Lord. Since we are all human and subjected daily to human influences, and since we universally employ comparison in establishing our meanings and values, we should be aware of some of those apparently innocent comparisons that blind us, misguide our intelligence, distort our sense of right, and lead us to destruction. May God help each of us to discover his own personal errors in this practice of comparing ourselves with others, to recognize the grave danger of such, and to seek a better course.

With the hope that some may be made more conscious of the personal handicap being suffered as a result of this practice, we shall review some of the many ways in which it is interfering with Christian growth and activity. That we may better understand, let us examine them against a Bible background. We now turn to the Bible teaching for information about such practices among the people of those days, and for standards by which to judge similar practices among us today.

In the days of Samuel, the elders of Israel came to him and said, "Behold thou art old and thy sons walk not in thy ways; now make us a king to judge us like all the nations" (I Sam. 8:4). In his distress, Samuel carried the matter to Jehovah. "And Jehovah said unto Samuel, Harken unto the voice of the people in all that they say unto thee; for they have not rejected thee, but they have rejected me, that I should not be king over them" (I Sam. 8:7). Why had those people rejected Jehovah? The answer is clear in their reply to Samuel's pleadings. "But the people refused to harken unto the voice of Samuel; and they said, Nay; but we will have a king over us, that we also may be like all the nations, and that our king may judge us, and go out before us, and fight our battles" (I Sam. 8:19-20). Here they say nothing about the wickedness of Samuel's sons, who had become judges, for that was beside the point. Their wickedness would have been reason for asking for other judges, but since the use of judges was God's order of government, it was not reason for wanting a king. So they rejected God that they might be like all the nations. How could they arrive at the point where their desire to be like the nations around them was strong enough to cause them to reject Jehovah, who had given them peace and success during the rule of Samuel, restoring to them the ark of the covenant and their possessions which had been held by the Philistines? They had lost their understanding by comparing themselves with the nations around about them. They were so blinded by the practice that they could reject God's way for man's way, reject God's wisdom for man's wisdom. As they beheld the glories of the nations with their king's courts and organizations, in contrast with the simple, unpretentious rule of the judges, had they decided that God's way was outmoded, that man's way was better? This is very unlikely. It is more reasonable to think that in their misunderstanding they were led to forget that the rule of judges was God's way and that they were seeking to replace it with their own. They had become ignorant, deceived, conceited to the point where they gave no heed to Samuel's pleadings. They probably contended with Samuel that they were not rejecting Jehovah, but God said, "They have rejected me, that I should not be king over them."

Is not this the case with us today? Do we not contend that we are following God's teaching? Would we dare to deliberately replace God's way by our own? Or have we not rather lost our understanding, become confused and misguided by our comparisons with the people around us until we fail to distinguish between divine wisdom and human wisdom? Does not every group of religious people claim to follow what the

Bible teaches, regardless of how many points of difference there are between it and all other denominations? Does not every conscientious member of any church group insist that he is a Christian, and that the Bible is his guide, even though he recognizes the fact that he disagrees with other people within and without his church group on much of the Bible teaching? Other groups have taken their liberty in changing God's Word so we do the same and think nothing about it. And since everybody seems to be doing it, we measure ourselves by them in this matter instead of measuring by God's Word. The idea seems to be that a man is acceptable before God if he is sincere in his belief that he is following God's Word. Thus, his faith is in his faith, and not in God. *We have not put our faith in God until we have placed his teaching above all other and honor and respect him by following it implicitly. This is the measure of our faith.*

Not only have we taken liberties with Bible interpretation because others have done the same, but we have adopted many personal practices and condoned many more because they are engaged in by people generally or by people who are considered religious. In this way church people on the average have ceased to measure their conduct by the Bible and have become so much like non-church people that the difference between the church and the world has been lost, and with it the respect of the world for the church is rapidly being lost.

Another way we are interpreting our Bible by what

people do is illustrated by the following. An elder of a congregation, "one in good standing," gave as his interpretation of the teaching "withdraw from those who walk disorderly," "withdraw from those who disturb the people of the congregation by introducing into the worship some practice that would cause division." He reasoned that it could not mean withdrawing from the person who continued to engage in misconduct or wicked practices because there were too many. If this is the way we are going to treat the Word of God, may the day come when we have enough respect for decency and common honesty to quit claiming to follow God's teaching.

Another place in which we have allowed human comparisons to vitiate Bible teaching is in our giving. Too frequently our contribution for a special need or our over-all contribution to the church is determined by what the people around us give. The question that is frequently asked when one is approached personally in raising money for some special need is, "What did Brother So-and-So give?" Thus, "liberally" and "as we have been prospered" have been replaced by "what others are doing." We seem to have forgotten that our giving is a measure of our loving, that the strength of our love is shown by a comparison of what we give with what we are able to give. As Jesus watched those who cast their gifts into the treasury he gave us the lesson. The widow who cast in only two mites cast in more than all the others (Luke 21:2-4). Yet in the measure that we apply, she cast in the least of all.

Thus, measuring ourselves by ourselves we are without understanding and the cause of our own Lord without adequate support.

Likewise, we justify our failure to study the Bible, our failure to attend worship, our failure to take part in the worship, our failure to do many deeds of kindness, our failure to encourage others in doing good and to discourage evil, and the most of our other failures, by measuring ourselves by others. Why are people able to justify themselves in so many different failures by this practice? Is it not because their selfish interests have led them to unreasonable or dishonest comparisons, unreasonable in selecting failures among men or dishonest in comparing only on points where they have the advantage?

Unreasonable comparison is not resorted to very frequently because its weakness is too easily observed by others. Sometimes one gives as his excuse for not becoming a Christian that he is better than the hypocrites in the church. But if the point is granted, it affords a very poor shield. Why select the failures? They have no promise of the things prepared for those who love God. Such comparisons are never made with those who are sincere in their efforts to follow God's way. Partial or dishonest comparisons are more common; hence, they should be considered more carefully.

While Jesus was eating in the house of Simon, the Pharisee, a woman came and washed Jesus' feet with her tears, dried them with her hair, anointed them, and kissed them. Simon condemned Jesus for allowing this sinner to touch him, but not for eating with him, which indicates that he considered himself better than the woman, and no doubt content with his behavior toward Jesus. But, he had not made a fair comparison. After giving the parable on forgiving and loving, Jesus said to Simon, "Seest thou this woman? I entered into thy house, thou gavest me no water for my feet: but she hath wetted my feet with her tears, and wiped them with her hair. Thou gavest me no kiss: but she, since the time I came in, hath not ceased to kiss my feet. My head with oil thou didst not anoint: but she hath anointed my feet with ointment. Wherefore I say unto thee, Her sins, which are many, are forgiven; for she loved much: but to whom little is forgiven, the same loveth little. And he said unto her, Thy sins are forgiven" (Luke 7:44-48). When Jesus made the comparison he gave Simon a different picture of himself. The same would be true many times with us if we compared on other points.

On another occasion the scribes and Pharisees brought a woman to Jesus who was taken in adultery and asked the question, "Now in the law Moses commanded us to stone such: what then sayest thou of her? And this they said, trying him, that they might have whereof to accuse him. But Jesus stooped down, and with his finger wrote on the ground. But when they continued asking him, he lifted up himself, and said unto them, He that is without sin among you, let him first cast a stone at her. And again he stooped down, and with his finger wrote on the ground. And they, when they heard it, went out one by one, beginning from the eldest, even unto the last: and Jesus was left alone, and the woman, where she was, in the midst. And Jesus lifted up himself, and said unto her, Woman, where are they? did no man condemn thee? And she said, No man, Lord. And Jesus said, Neither do I condemn thee: go thy way; from henceforth sin no more" (John 8:5-11). Why did these men who had pressed Jesus for an answer to their question leave without it? As they compared themselves with the woman on the point of adultery they thought well of themselves, but when Jesus presented the full standard of measure they got a different picture of themselves and were so embarrassed they sneaked away. They had been measuring themselves by the woman's weakness and not by God's Word. This measuring by another person's weaknesses and failings is our most dangerous practice today.

The more we do it the more we become like the Pharisee of Jesus' parable who went up into the temple to pray. "The Pharisee stood and prayed thus with himself, God, I thank thee, that I am not as the rest of men, extortioners, unjust, adulterers, or even as this publican. I fast twice in the week; I give tithes of all that I get" (Luke 18:11-12). We should seek the attitude of the publican who recognized his failure. "But the publican, standing afar off, would not lift up so much as his eyes unto heaven, but smote his breast, saying, God, be thou merciful to me a sinner" (Luke 18:13). If we will measure ourselves by God's teaching,

we will recognize our weaknesses and have that attitude.

In his warning to his disciples, Jesus gave us a very
graphic picture of the pitiable plight to which one may
come by this practice. "And why beholdest thou the
mote that is in thy brother's eye, but considerest not
the beam that is in thine own eye? Or how wilt thou
say to thy brother, Let me cast out the mote out of
thine eye; and lo, the beam is in thine own eye? Thou
hypocrite, cast out first the beam out of thine own eye;
and then shalt thou see clearly to cast out the mote
out of thy brother's eye" (Matt. 7:3-5). How many of
us have lost our understanding and dwarfed our
development by becoming "mote hunters"?

Jesus also warned against considering the misfortunes
of others as marks of sinfulness and by comparison
justifying oneself. "Now there were some present at
that very season who told him of the Galileans, whose
blood Pilate had mingled with their sacrifices. And he
answered and said unto them, Think ye that these
Galilaeans were sinners above all the Galilaeans, because they have suffered these things? I tell you, Nay:
but, except ye repent, ye shall all in like manner perish.
Or those eighteen, upon whom the tower in Siloam
fell, and killed them, think ye that they were offenders
above all the men that dwell in Jerusalem? I tell you,
Nay: but, except ye repent, ye shall all likewise perish"
(Luke 13:1-5). Echoes of this practice are heard
occasionally today in attributing floods, earthquakes,
or fires to the sinfulness of the people of those sections

where they occur. Also sometimes the idea is implied by the use of these words in prayer, "Father, we thank thee that we have no mark of thy displeasure upon us."

All of the ways in which this practice of comparing ourselves with others leads to religious failure cannot be included in this discussion. There is one other, however, somewhat different in its method of operation, that must not be overlooked, for the very nature of its operation makes it the more dangerous.

It is the practice of overestimating our spiritual strength in withstanding temptation. The fall of thousands of other people under certain conditions is no warning to us because we think we are strong enough to resist. The fact that thousands of boys and girls, men and women, have begun their unvirtuous lives at necking parties or on the dance floor is no warning. The fact that thousands of gamblers began their career at the card table is no warning. The fact that thousands of people began their lives of crime by their association with the wrong class of people is no warning. *Why?* Simply because each of us thinks he is stronger than the man who failed. Thus, we are just strong enough to be weak enough to ignore the danger of playing with fire. So we ignore all of the warnings as unworthy of consideration.

If you are interested in a personal checkup, apply the following questions to yourself.

1. Do you unnecessarily expose yourself to temptations that have proven too much for others?
2. Do you assume that all is well because you have suffered no evil that can be attributed to divine displeasure?

3. Do you adjudge yourself better than another because of some particular weakness he might have?

4. Do you justify your failures by the idea that many others are doing no better?

5. Do you consider a practice right because it is common or is indulged in by respected religious people?

6. Do you decide what you will give by what your neighbor gives?

7. Do you interpret any Bible teaching as you do because of existing conditions?

8. Do you remain content with your interpretation of Bible teaching because of the existence of so many diverse views?

If your answer to any of these questions is *yes,* beware! You are measuring yourself by others and not by the Bible and in danger of being without understanding and losing your soul.

QUESTIONS ON LECTURE VII

1. Name the three interrelated factors that we have studied thus far.

2. Show how these three factors form a vicious circle.

3. The important question is not how much can you tell your neighbor, but what?

4. Name the three facts that we are to consider about the Corinthians.

5. Why was it so bad to be without understanding?

6. Name some of the practices of the Corinthians that indicated that they were without understanding.

7. What had they been doing that caused them to be without understanding?

8. What was their attitude toward themselves that showed that they were without understanding?

9. Show how we have followed this practice of comparing ourselves with others since childhood.

10. What is our purpose in using such?
11. What practice were they following that no human being with understanding would follow?
12. By what is our vicious circle driven?
13. What is the vicious circle within the vicious circle?
14. Illustrate this from the field of religious differences.
15. What should we never lose sight of in regard to these human weaknesses?
16. Into what trouble did this practice lead the Jews in the days of Samuel?
17. Show a similarity between the way the people of Israel rejected Jehovah and many people of today are rejecting him.
18. Illustrate this practice in the field of personal practices, interpretation of Bible teaching, giving, attending church, studying the Bible, etc.
19. What unreasonable comparison do we sometimes hear made?
20. Show how the case of Simon, that of the woman taken in adultery, that of the Pharisee in the temple illustrate this practice.
21. Give Jesus' picture of the pitiable plight to which one may come by this practice.
22. By what illustration did Jesus warn against considering misfortunes of others marks of greater sinfulness?
23. What is the great danger of over-estimating our spiritual strength?

LECTURE VIII

WHY THE JEWS REJECTED JESUS

THE causes of failure to understand or agree with the New Testament teaching today are the same as those of the days of Jesus and the apostles. This is one of the major assumptions with which this series of lessons was begun. An examination of the New Testament scriptures has shown us unmistakably that the basic cause for the rejection of Jesus' teaching among both Jews and Gentiles during the time of Jesus' ministry and that of the apostles was ignorance. Thus far our study of those factors which are responsible for ignorance of God's teaching has not been primarily concerned with specific application to the people of Jesus' day, but rather a general examination of the human weaknesses clearly delineated in the New Testament through which man has been led into ignorance and by which he continues in ignorance. This plan of study has been followed with the hope that we might better understand why the people of New Testament times, many of whom witnessed the miracles of Jesus and the apostles, remained in ignorance, refusing to accept Jesus' teaching as the truth. Trusting that our background has been reasonably well prepared, we shall now further examine the question as it applied to the people of the first century of the Christian era. We shall give attention to the Jews first.

113

After John the Baptist had been imprisoned, he heard of the wonderful works which Jesus did and sent his disciples to him with this question, "Art thou he that cometh, or look we for another?" (Matt. 11:3). Jesus answered their question, and as they went away Jesus said many things to the multitude concerning John, closing his description with this statement, "And if ye are willing to receive it, this is Elijah, that is to come" (Matt. 11:14). This expression, "if ye are willing to receive it," suggests that Jesus knew that there were many people who were not willing. The fact that some would not accept this simple statement is further implied by Jesus' admonition which immediately followed. "He that hath ears to hear, let him hear" (Matt. 11:15). Why would they be unwilling to accept Jesus' statement that John the Baptist was the Elijah that was to come? It was for the same reason that they had rejected Jesus.

Let us now look at Jesus' picture of the Jews of his day that had rejected him. It consists of a parable, two illustrations, and a statement of principle. As is true of all parables, this one sets forth one major point. The one thing shown in this parable is the human element in the people of that day which was responsible not only for their rejecting John the Baptist, but for their rejection of Jesus himself. Jesus introduces his parable with the question, "But whereunto shall I liken this generation?" That is, what is there to which I may compare these people that will give you an understanding of what caused them to reject the truth?

The parable is given in answer. "It (this generation) is like unto children sitting in the marketplaces, who call unto their fellows and say, We piped unto you, and ye did not dance; we wailed, and ye did not mourn" (Matt. 11:16-17). Jesus tells us that the people of that generation were like children. In what way were they like children? Were they humble like those innocent, unambitious, trusting little children whom Jesus said we must all come to resemble if we enter the kingdom of heaven (Matt. 18:3)? The description in the parable is just the opposite. Let us examine it closely.

The children are described as sitting in the marketplaces. No play is going on. Children normally play. This is an unnatural situation in itself and suggests that Jesus is describing an abnormal condition among those people as the cause of their unwillingness to hear. The unique statement of the parable lends further emphasis to the same thing. It is not related in direct narrative form. The body of the story is indirectly given through a brief statement of the negative results expressed by the participants in such a way as to throw personal factors into bold relief. They call to their fellows (or as Luke says, "call one to another"), "we piped unto you and ye did not dance; we wailed and ye did not mourn." The picture is one of rugged individualism, a picture of selfish stubbornness or stubborn selfishness. They wanted their own way. They wanted to direct themselves. They were unwilling to act upon the ideas of another. They were first offered the game of joy and merrymaking, one that gives expression to the lighter emotions, the wedding procession or feast, but they would not play. Then the game that provides activity for the more somber emotion, the funeral procession or burial, was proposed, but it was also rejected. Their refusal was not caused by the character of the game suggested but by their own personal attitude. They wanted to do what they wanted to do and were unwilling to yield to another. They were in bondage to their own ideas. Immediately after finishing this parable, Jesus reinforces this lesson by illustrating from the lives of the people about whom he is talking.

The first case is that of John the Baptist. "For John came neither eating nor drinking, and they say, He hath a demon" (Matt. 11:18). John was not only born of priestly lineage (Luke 1:5), but was also a Nazarite (Luke 1:15). He wore the dress of a prophet and ate a simple food. He abstained from strong drink and other fleshly indulgences and taught the people to turn away from their wicked and selfish way of living, accepting the baptism of repentance in preparation for him who was to come. These teachings were so foreign to their ideas and so antagonistic to their practices, and, being blinded by their own conceit, their thinking had become so distorted that they not only rejected John but justified their rejection by the rationalization that he had a demon. They were probably further strengthened in their rejection of John by their misunderstanding of the prophecy of Malachi. It seemed that they had interpreted the prophecy literally and expected Elijah, the Tishbite, the one who was taken up into heaven in a whirlwind, to return before the day of the Messiah. When they asked John if he were Elijah in person, his answer was "No." And thus their overconfidence in their own wisdom caused them to reject for themselves the counsel of God, being not baptized of John (Luke 7:30).

Jesus' next illustration is that of himself. "The Son of man came eating and drinking, and they say, Behold, a gluttonous man and a winebibber, a friend of publicans and sinners" (Matt. 11:19). Jesus came teaching the same principles of upright living as those taught by John, but he was not born of a priestly trible nor was he under the Nazarite vow. Hence, his food and dress did not vary widely from that of the other people of his day. Thus, since there was nothing in his daily life sufficiently radical to justify their reasoning in making such a charge against him as they had made against John, they exaggerated his manner of living and misrepresented his social life, classifying him with the rabble. They rejected John because he abstained from the common practices of the day and rejected Jesus because he followed them.

Jesus closes his discussion of these people by stating their difficulty in the form of a principle, "And wisdom is justified by her works" (Matt. 11:19). The usual discussion of this passage by commentators considers this a statement of a general principle that the wisdom of the action in which one has engaged is determined by the fruit or the result. Some add, with reference to the foregoing illustrative material, that those who were wise justified the conduct of both John and Jesus. Those who rejected them, of course, were unwise. Since this statement is spoken in such close relationship to the foregoing parable and illustrative material which we have studied, it seems that its interpretation should show a closer relationship to this immediate discussion, of which it appears to be the conclusion. Certainly no action can be considered the part of wisdom unless the result therefrom is considered satisfactory. But this does not bar the influence of deceit in judging the results. One may be deceived and think that the result of his decision or action is right and good when it is not, but so long as this is the case, he remains confident in his own wisdom, as Paul would say, "Wise in his own conceit." The wise man shows the extreme to which this may be practiced when he says, "The way of a fool is right in his own eyes" (Prov. 12:15). This is precisely the case of the people whom Jesus had been describing. They had rejected John; they had also rejected Jesus and in each case had justified their own decision and were still confident in their own wisdom. In their wisdom, these people had rejected the baptism of John and were perfectly satisfied that their action was the part of wisdom, but Jesus states that in doing so, "They rejected for themselves the counsel of God" (Luke 7:30). Of course, Jesus was not speaking of the mere formal act of baptism, but that they had refused John's teaching, had refused to prepare for, as well as to accept, the baptism of repentance. Is it not true

today that many people are following the same course
as that of the Pharisees and for the same reason—because they have become wise in their own conceit?

If the Pharisees and lawyers rejected for themselves
the counsel of God by not being baptized of John, is
it not true today that when people refuse to accept the
baptism taught by Jesus and his apostles they are rejecting for themselves the counsel of God? Jesus tells
us plainly that his teaching is not his but the Father's
who sent him. After his resurrection from the dead, he
declared to the disciples, "All authority hath been given
unto me in heaven and on earth" (Matt. 28:18). And
then charged them, "Go ye therefore, and make disciples of all the nations, baptizing them into the name
of the Father and of the Son and of the Holy Spirit:
teaching them to observe all things whatsoever I commanded you" (Matt. 28:19-20). His disciples followed
this. Were they not following the counsel of God?
Can we reject it without rejecting the counsel of God?
Of course, the practice of accepting baptism as a form
and apart from the rest of Jesus' teaching is not accepting the counsel of God. It would only become such
when one has been led by faith in Jesus' teaching to
the recognition of the fact that he is a sinner and
caused to change his attitude from that of an enemy
to that of a friend, being reconciled to God through
the love of God which was shown in the sacrifice of his
Son, and in godly sorrow turning away from those
things which displease God, confessing Jesus to be the
Son of God and accepting him as his Lord.

In talking about these same people in the Roman letter, comparing them with the Gentiles, Paul tells us why they failed to attain unto that righteousness which is by faith. "What shall we say then? That the Gentiles, who followed not after righteousness, attained to righteousness, even the righteousness which is of faith: but Israel, following after a law of righteousness, did not arrive at that law. Wherefore? Because they sought it not by faith, but as it were by works" (Rom. 9:30-32). Why did the Jews fail? Because "they sought it not by faith, but as it were, by works." It seems that their faith in the righteousness of God had ceased, and they had come to trust in their own righteousness. They had failed to see the law as an opportunity to show their faith in God, but rather put their trust in their own ability to comply with the demands of the law. Thus their emphasis came to be placed upon form and ritual and this misplaced emphasis so distorted the law, that it failed in its function as a tutor to lead them to Christ. Thus Paul writes, "They stumbled at the stone of stumbling; even as it is written, Behold, I lay in Zion a stone of stumbling and a rock of offence: And he that believeth on him shall not be put to shame" (Rom. 9:32-33). Their failure was not due to indifference. Paul says, "For I bear them witness that they have a zeal for God, but not according to knowledge. For being ignorant of God's righteousness, and seeking to establish their own" (Rom. 10:2-3). They trusted in their own works. We should be careful today lest we fall by the same error. We should always remember

that baptism, worship, purity of life, are not faith, but
the expressions of faith. We may comply with some of
these forms without faith, but if we have a sincere
faith in God we will not willingly neglect his counsel
on any point.

Jesus, in explaining to his disciples why he spake to
the multitudes in parables, quoted to them the description that had been given of these people by Isaiah the
prophet. "And unto them is fulfilled the prophecy of
Isaiah, which saith, By hearing ye shall hear, and shall
in no wise understand; And seeing ye shall see, and
shall in no wise perceive: For this people's heart is
waxed gross, And their ears are dull of hearing, And
their eyes they have closed; Lest haply they should
perceive with their eyes, And hear with their ears,
And understand with their heart, And should turn again,
And I should heal them" (Matt. 13:14-15). Paul quotes
the same description to those that were chief of the
Jews in Rome when after a day of reasoning concerning
Jesus many of them had rejected his teaching (Acts
28:26-27). Here again we find the self-satisfaction of
the people given as the cause of their hearing and not
understanding and seeing and not perceiving. "For
this people's heart is waxed gross." Figuratively speaking, their heart was enlarged. They had come to have
too much self-satisfaction, self-confidence, self-conceit.

Some might object that John refers to the same
prophecy of Isaiah and tells us that they could not
believe because they must fulfill the prophecy. "For
this cause they could not believe, for that Isaiah said

again, He hath blinded their eyes, and he hardened their heart; Lest they should see with their eyes, and perceive with their heart, And should turn, And I should heal them" (John 12:39-40). Therefore, their personal qualities were not the determining factors. However, John goes on to say, "Nevertheless even of the rulers many believed on him; but because of the Pharisees they did not confess it, lest they should be put out of the synagogue" (John 12:42). The first part of this statement, certainly when considered along with Jesus' and Paul's application of Isaiah's prophecy, indicates that it was a general description of those people and not an idea of individual predestination. Recall the fact that Paul used it in talking with a group of Jews of whom some had believed.

Jesus pointed out the same weakness in other groups of the Jews. On one occasion, he was talking with some who had rejoiced for a while in the teaching of John the Baptist. They were the ones to whom he said, "Ye search the scriptures, because ye think that in them ye have eternal life; and these are they which bear witness of me; and ye will not come to me, that ye may have life" (John 5:39-40). After stating their troubles thus, "I know you, that ye have not the love of God in yourselves" (John 5:42), he divulges the cause for it all in his question, "How can ye believe, who receive glory one of another, and the glory that cometh from the only God ye seek not?" (John 5:44). Seeking the glory of men is an effort at self-exaltation and a sure sign of pride and self-conceit. Seeking the glory of men rather than the glory of God likewise is un-mistakable evidence that people are deceived to the point of blindness and continue content with their ignorance.

Is this not enough to warn everyone of us against the practice of allowing the ideas which we now hold to become blinding to us and preventing our coming to a full knowledge of the truth? Is it not true that many of our ideas upon matters of Christian living, as well as upon matters of church organization and worship, were accepted from our leaders and teachers in the days of our ignorance, as was true in the case of the Jews? Have we ever taken the time to carefully re-evaluate them in the light of the New Testament teaching? Can we afford to go on blindly this way? My plea is that we stop putting our trust in the words of men and place it in the words of God, take the time to honestly and thoughtfully study the Bible in that humble attitude which is imperative if we are to free ourselves from the shackles of self-conceit.

QUESTIONS ON LECTURE VIII

1. With what condition did Jesus preface his statement that John was the Elijah that was to come?
2. The picture that Jesus gave of the Jews consists of what four things?
3. With what did Jesus compare the people of his day?
4. What characteristic of children were they like?
5. Why did the children not play?
6. What illustrations did Jesus use to show that many of the Jews had acted like these children?

7. How did the people justify themselves in rejecting John?
8. How had they probably been further strengthened in their rejection of John?
9. How did they justify their rejection of Jesus?
10. In what principle does Jesus sum up the difficulty of these people?
11. How have many commentators interpreted this statement?
12. What may cause one to judge his act to be that of wisdom when it is not?
13. Give the statement of the wise man that shows the extreme to which this may be practiced.
14. What implies that the Jews thought that they had acted wisely in rejecting both John and Jesus?
15. What had they rejected when they rejected the baptism of John?
16. What was evidently included in this rejection?
17. What are we rejecting when we reject Jesus' baptism?
18. Under what conditions does accepting Jesus' baptism become a true acceptance of the counsel of God?
19. Why did the Jews fail to attain unto that righteousness which is by faith?
20. Why had the law failed to lead these people to Christ?
21. At what had they stumbled?
22. What evidence do we have that their trouble was not indifference?
23. What should we always remember that we may avoid the same sort of mistake?
24. What phrase did Isaiah use in describing the conceitedness of these people?
25. What indicates that these people rejected because of their own personal qualities?
26. How did Jesus explain the trouble to those, who for a while had rejoiced in the teaching of John?
27. What warning should we take from this teaching?

THE WISDOM OF MEN VERSUS
THE WISDOM OF GOD

IN our study of why the people of Jesus' day and the days of the apostles held varied ideas about Jesus' teaching, the major attention naturally has been given to the causes among the Jews. This is due to the fact that the record provides a more detailed analysis of the Jewish people and their difficulties. Since these were the people with whom Jesus and the apostles were more closely associated in their work of teaching the truth, we shall turn next to an overall picture sketched by the apostle Paul in his first letter to the Corinthian people.

First, Paul divides the people of his day into two general classes and shows their respective attitudes toward God's teaching. "For the word of the cross is to them that perish foolishness; but unto us who are saved it is the power of God" (I Cor. 1:18). With this he introduces the topic of wisdom and foolishness. As he continues his discussion, he makes it clear that as those that perish have adjudged God's teaching to be foolishness, God has observed that man's wisdom is foolishness. It seems that God considered man's wisdom foolishness because through it men did not come to know God as Paul declared, "For seeing that in the wisdom of God the world through its wisdom knew

not God, it was God's good pleasure through the foolishness of the preaching to save them that believe" (1 Cor.
1:21). In this verse we are also given God's solution
to the problem. Since man through his wisdom would
never know God, it was God's good pleasure to offer his
wisdom to man through preaching, which man considered foolishness, and to save them that believe.
There are millions today who still admittedly consider
preaching foolishness and ignore it completely. There
are probably millions of others who through social or
other influences have been led to "profess that they
know God," to whom preaching or study of God's Word
seems yet to be only foolishness. As Paul spake of the
Jews, "For being ignorant of God's righteousness, and
seeking to establish their own, they did not subject
themselves to the righteousness of God" (Rom. 10:3).
So they have not received through preaching or study
God's wisdom and, therefore, are still following their
own human wisdom.

After showing that the great human difficulty with
respect to accepting God's wisdom is dethroning of
human wisdom (with which it does not harmonize),
Paul breaks down his classification to show that the
cases of Jews and Gentiles, though basically the same,
are characteristically different. "Seeing that Jews ask
for signs, and Greeks seek after wisdom: but we preach
Christ crucified, unto Jews a stumbling-block, and unto
Gentiles foolishness; but unto them that are called, both
Jews and Greeks, Christ the power of God, and the
wisdom of God" (I Cor. 1:22-24).

After stating the dominating activity of the Jews and Greeks generally, asking signs and seeking after wisdom, Paul shows that "Christ crucified" has three diverse meanings to three different classes of people. What accounts for the difference? Why was "Christ crucified" a stumbling block to the Jews? The Jews had been taught of the coming Messiah. They knew that he was to be of the lineage of David. They knew that he was to be born in Bethlehem. They knew that he was to be born of a virgin. They were looking forward to his coming. Then when Jesus of Nazareth fulfilled these and many other teachings, why was he rejected? They had been taught that he would sit upon the literal throne of David and restore the kingdom to Israel. This erroneous teaching had been taught them from youth, and was so wholeheartedly believed that it dominated their thinking and blinded them to any teaching that was not in accord with it. "Christ crucified" was directly opposed to the expectation of the Jews. If he were to be crucified he could not sit on the throne of David and restore the earthly kingdom to Israel; hence, the teaching was a stumbling block at which many of the Jews fell.

In the case of the apostle Peter, we have an illustration of the effect of this teaching. After associating with Jesus for many months, seeing his miracles, hearing his teaching and confessing him to be the Son of the living God, when he was told plainly that Jesus was going to be crucified, he denied that it would ever happen, saying, "Be it far from thee, Lord: this shall

never be unto thee" (Matt. 16:22).   He was still cling-
ing tenaciously to the idea that had been instilled in
him by his teachers of earlier days, that the Messiah
would sit upon the literal throne of David. What was
the matter with Peter?   How could he confess Jesus
to be the Son of God and immediately afterward, or
in a short time at most, deny the truthfulness of his
statement? Jesus answered the question in his rebuke
to Peter. "But he turned, and said unto Peter, Get thee
behind me, Satan: thou art a stumbling-block unto me:
for thou mindest not the things of God, but the things
of men" (Matt. 16:23).   Yes, Peter, though he had
sincerely and unreservedly confessed Jesus to be the
Christ, was holding to his former erroneous teaching
which led him to reject Jesus' teaching on this point.

Since this was the case with Peter who had been
closely associated with his Lord, it should not be surprising that many people today confess Jesus to be the
Christ and reject part of his teaching because of
erroneous ideas which they have acquired formerly.
This is the way a man becomes blinded and enslaved
to his own ideas; being ignorant of God's teaching he
mistakes his own for God's and zealously follows it
with confidence and ill-founded assurance. In this
way our religious error continues to be zealously
propagated. Now for the sake of God's honor, the influence upon man, and your own soul's salvation, do
not hear these words and say, "Yes, that is right, that
is just the reason other people do not agree with me
on this or that."   You are human and whether your

pride will allow you to admit it or not you are subject to this same weakness, and the chances are far more than equal that in some of your practices you come under the rebuke, "thou mindest not the things of God but the things of men."

Just how many and of what magnitude may be the errors practiced by a conscientious person without falling under the condemnation of the Almighty, I do not know. (You may.) Just which type of error man can continue to practice and be forgiven and which type will not be forgiven, I am not able to tell. (You may.) I am confident, however, that there are few individuals that are not practicing error of some sort and that we are all far more dependent upon the mercy of God than we have ever realized. Also, I am fully persuaded that the care which we exercise in studying God's Word to learn what he would have us do and how he would have us do it is just as surely an evidence of our love for God as the zeal with which we practice the teachings which we believe to be his. A failure to study is a failure to respect his authority and a failure to honor his wisdom.

In the case of the Gentiles, why did they consider "Christ crucified" as foolishness? Because they were seeking wisdom. They had no false ideas about the work and teaching of the Messiah as did the Jews, but when measured by their human standards it simply did not make sense for the savior of mankind to be subject to the forces of nature. If he could not save himself, how could he save others? How could one with the power, the wisdom and the glory that they would ascribe to a savior come to such an ignominious death as the one that Jesus died upon the cross? This, to them, was a mark of inferiority rather than one of superiority. Then how could a man be a savior of man? Furthermore, they were not acquainted with God's ways nor his teaching, and since God worked through the avenue of human agency and since sorcery and witchcraft was widely practiced, it was easy to attribute God's accomplishment to the human agency.

In brief, "Christ crucified" just did not fit into their system of thought as an evidence that he was the Son of God and the savior of the world. Thus, so long as they clung blindly to their own human ideas or philosophy and reasoned from their own worldly mental content, the teaching appeared unto them as foolishness. Therefore, so long as they were deceived into believing that they knew, so long as they were wise in their own conceits, they remained ignorant and refused the teaching of the Son of God. This is illustrated by the philosophers to whom Paul spake in the Areopagus at Athens. They were content to listen so long as he reasoned of those things within the material comparisons of life, but when Paul declared the resurrection from the dead to be the assuring evidence unto all men, most of the philosophers refused to listen longer (Acts 17:31-32).

Why had both Jews and Gentiles rejected the word of the cross? Because of their ignorance. Why were they ignorant? Not because of lack of intelligence or lack of general education, but because they were blinded and deceived by their own ideas and they were bound to these ideas by their self-confidence or conceit. The Jews' erroneous ideas of God's teaching—that God would establish an earthly kingdom—branded as untenable the doctrine of the crucifixion. The Gentiles' idea of wisdom, which was the product of their own restricted human experience, pronounced the doctrine of the crucifixion wholly incompatible with sound reason and, therefore, considered it foolishness. In their pride as descendents of Abraham, God's chosen people, the Jews had become conceited and so much were they blinded by their own self-confidence that a teaching to the contrary received no consideration. In their pride as the leaders of human thought, the Gentiles had become blinded through earthly wisdom and thus were wholly incapable of arriving at a spiritual conclusion through the use of their materialistic thoughts.

In these two peoples we have represented the two major conditions which cause people not to see the Bible alike today. The first, represented by the Jews, is the practice of holding to erroneous religious ideas, or probably more correctly stated, of being held by erroneous religious ideas. The second, represented by the Gentiles, is the incapacitation for accepting spiritual teaching due to a materialistic mental content. The former is probably the most important cause among religious people and the latter among the non-religious people. However, the close association of many religious people with materialism and the limited association with God's Word is having its effects upon their interpretation or misinterpretation of Bible ideas. This seems to be a source of religious difficulty especially among the young people who attend our secular colleges and universities. The professors do not generally make direct attacks upon the students' religious convictions, at least not until the students' religious thought content has been largely changed from spiritual to material. This change is brought about gradually by the method of association. The student, due to the time required by his college studies and that consumed by his extra-curricula and social activities, spends little or no time with spiritual teaching. Thus, his spiritual thoughts are replaced by material and so his spiritual life is stifled and his understanding of spiritual things is terribly distorted or completely lost. One cannot put together material thoughts and arrive at a spiritual conclusion any more readily than he can put together concrete blocks and construct a brick house. This same thing can happen to those in less virile materialistic environment where spiritual influences are unheeded.

We have seen how the erroneous religious ideas of the Jews made "Christ crucified" a stumbling block to them, and the worldly ideas of the Greeks made "Christ crucified" foolishness to them. We should not conclude, however, that the mere possession of incorrect information, in the respective cases, had through its power made prisoners of those who possessed it by taking away their freedom of action. This is evident from the latter part of Paul's statement, "But unto them that are called, both Jews and Greeks, Christ the power of God, and the wisdom of God" (I Cor. 1:24). There were those from each class who had accepted the truth. Undoubtedly, those who were Jews had believed the false teaching of the Jews, and those who were Gentiles had shared in the worldly ideas of the Gentiles. Then why did they accept Christ as "the power of God, and the wisdom of God," while others who held the same erroneous ideas considered his teaching foolishness? Since all had been incorrectly taught and some changed while others did not, it is clear that man's refusal to give up error when the truth is presented is not chargeable to the fact that he has been formerly given incorrect ideas. If this were true, the case would be hopeless. Then what is responsible for the difference? Why does error hold some people and not others? Is not man's attitude toward the error the determining factor? This question is not, "Does he believe or not believe the idea to be correct?" Certainly the degree of confidence one has in the soundness of any idea, or the conviction he has that a statement is true, is important in determining the readiness with which an intelligent person will accept a teaching and the tenacity with which he will cling to it. The question is how much personal value does the idea hold for that individual? How closely is it interwoven into his system of thought or how vitally is it interlocked with the practices and relationships of life that are dear to him? How many friends and relatives share the idea with him? Ideas as well as objects and relationships that give us great satisfaction or enjoyment are cherished.

This is his measure of their worth. Things that are not related to one's happiness are not evaluated very highly and are given up more easily. On the other hand, those things that give great satisfaction or enjoyment, people are loath to give up. This is true of ideas as well as objects and relationships. Consider this illustration. If a watch does not keep correct time, is not sufficiently beautiful or unique to give us pride in showing it to others, or does not serve to remind us of sacred memories, it is of little value and is likely to be disposed of or discarded. If it furnishes either of these satisfactions, it will not be discarded. If it affords all of them, it will be considered very valuable, guarded closely, and given up only when one is forced to do so. The case of an idea or a teaching is similar. If, it serves to justify a practice which one enjoys, or relieves from a responsibility that would be burdensome, or permits a freedom which one craves, it will be given up reluctantly. Or, if one has made it a part of himself by practicing it before his fellows, or contending for it in public and thereby enjoying the praise of those who agree with him, he will relinquish it with difficulty. If the teaching has been received from those whom one holds in high esteem, practiced by one's relatives and friends, and especially if it is a vital element in those happy associations that give meaning to life, it is seldom repudiated. If all these conditions exist, one is bound to the teaching with a fetter that will not likely be broken. These are some of the ways incorrect teaching has acquired personal value and has come to have the power to bind one to it as a slave to his master. There is an added danger to be found in the very nature of the case. The more strongly one becomes attached to error the more blinded he is to truth and the less capable of judging between truth and error, and the more helpless and the more hopeless his case becomes.

Were the physician to picture to you the horrors and the grim fatality of the dreaded malady of cancer, point out to you the shocking increase in the spread of this deadly enemy of human life, inform you that it is occurring in families without relation to hereditary background or to human body type, remind you of the fact that medical science can do nothing unless the trouble is discovered early, provide you with a list of symptoms that indicate its presence, and warn you that general feeling of health and well-being is no assurance that malignancy is not already taking root in the vital organs of your body, would you be indifferent to the physician's plea to get acquainted with the symptoms and make a personal checkup? Surely, you would not!

Listener, whoever you are, regardless of your religious convictions, your church affiliations, or the level of your spiritual development, for the safety of your own soul and for the glory of God, do not fail to give consideration to these warnings. You are human and subject to these blighting human weaknesses that threaten your life for eternity more surely than fleshly maladies threaten your life for time. They may be, at this very moment, gnawing at the very vitals of your spiritual existence while you are contented or even happy in your self-satisfaction. This is not a plea against any church group or individual. It is not a plea for any personal favor or honor. It is not a plea that you support some cause, human or otherwise. It is a solicitation for your soul. "And if ye call on him as Father, who without respect of persons judgeth according to each man's work, pass the time of your sojourning in fear" (I Pet. 1:17).

QUESTIONS ON LECTURE IX

1. Into what two general classes does Paul divide the people?
2. What will man never come to know through his own wisdom?
3. What evidence do we have today that people still consider preaching foolishness?
4. "Christ crucified" was what three things to what three classes of people?
5. Why was "Christ crucified" a stumbling block to the Jews?
6. Illustrate this with the case of the apostle Peter.
7. How does a man become blinded and enslaved to his own ideas?
8. What is pointed out as a failure to respect God's authority and to honor his wisdom?
9. Why did the Gentiles consider "Christ crucified" foolishness?
10. Illustrate this from Paul's speech at Athens.
11. Why did both Jews and Gentiles reject the word of the cross?
12. What two major conditions of today do we have represented in these two peoples that cause people not to see the Bible alike?

13. What is probably more correct than the expression "holding erroneous religious ideas"?
14. How are young people caused to lose their religious convictions during their college attendance?
15. What evidence do we have that both Jews and Gentiles could change?
16. Why does error hold some people and not others?
17. What is the measure of the worth of things? Illustrate.
18. What relationships generally tie people to their religious ideas?

THE NATURE OF THE BIBLE TEACHING

IN the preceding discussions of "Why Do People Not See the Bible Alike?" our attention has been given largely to those human weaknesses, ignorance, deception, and conceit, that are not only responsible for people's failure to understand the Bible but also for the misdirected zeal of many in teaching their misconceptions. While these personal weaknesses have been and are the most insidious hindrances to a correct understanding of Bible teaching, there are others that have contributed and are continuing to contribute to man's failure to comprehend God's Word. Not least among them is the failure to be mindful of the nature and organization of the Bible.

In order to properly understand God's teaching to us, it is necessary that we view the entire Bible as one teaching with a certain unity and continuity of thought from Genesis through Revelation. At the same time, it is equally important that we recognize a definite individuality of teaching to the people of the different periods of Bible history. Thus to deal with the Bible as one teaching without giving due consideration to the detailed changes from one dispensation to another will result in misinterpretations. Likewise, dissecting the Bible and over-stressing some particular period to the neglect of the whole Bible teaching will give rise to another set of misinterpretations. This implies that there must be a proper balance of emphasis, and thus suggests a very fertile field of human variation. Hence, it should not be surprising that many of our differences in Bible interpretation, both denominational and individual, have their origin in part in this variation of emphasis. Some people have stressed the Bible teaching as given to man under the various dispensations to the neglect of the broader view of Bible teaching, while others have contented themselves with Bible teaching generally and minimized the importance placed upon the specific instruction to the people in the different periods of Bible history.

May we draw an illustration from the field of music. When a string of a musical instrument is plucked it vibrates as a whole, from end to end, providing the basic tone of the string. It also, at the same time, vibrates in sections or parts causing other sounds, called partials or overtones, that blend with the basic tone to make up the true sound of the string. Suppose some conditions could be arranged under which one could hear the overtones or partials, but could not hear the basic tone. He would not hear the true tone of the string. Suppose conditions were arranged so that one could hear the basic tone of the string, but could not hear the overtones or partials. He would not hear the true tone of the string. Or if either the basic tone or an overtone were heard with reduced strength the true tone of the string would not be heard. In our Bible study we have a similar situation. The great lessons on God's nature and his expectation of man, taught by precept and example throughout the full scope of the Bible, correspond to the basic tone of the string. The teaching to any dispensation, Patriarchal, Mosaic, or Christian, harmonizes with the great basic lessons of the whole Bible and correspond to the partials or overtones of the string that result from its sectional vibration. Unless all are given their proper consideration, the harmony of the Bible teaching is distorted and God's teaching is misunderstood.

In the hope of arriving at a better understanding of the effect of this misplaced emphasis upon our interpretations of Bible teachings, we shall now give some thought to the nature of the book.

The first thing that should be borne in mind by one who would understand the teaching is the fact that it is the revelation of the one God. It is the portrayal of an unchanging God to an ever-changing world. God himself declared, "For I, Jehovah, change not." (Mal. 3:6.) Though human conditions, customs, and practices have varied with passing generations, the God of the Bible is the same from the earliest record of Genesis to the final word in Revelation, and will continue to be so. The God whom we serve is the same in every attribute as the God of the Jews. Our God is truly the God of Abraham, of Isaac, and of Jacob. Through his dealing with men and through his teaching from generation to generation, he has shown himself to be the God of power, of wisdom, and of glory; the God of love, of mercy, and of compassion; the God of vengeance, of terror, and of destruction.

God has not revealed himself as a God of severity to the peoples of the Old Testament days and a God of goodness and mercy to the people of the present period. He was equally good to the earlier generations as to the later. On Mount Horeb, God declared it unto Moses, "And Jehovah passed by before him, and proclaimed, Jehovah, Jehovah, a God merciful and gracious, slow to anger, and abundant in lovingkindness and truth; keeping lovingkindness for thousands, forgiving iniquity and transgression and sin; and that will by no means clear the guilty, visiting the iniquity of the fathers upon the children, and upon the children's children, upon the third and upon the fourth generation." (Exod. 34:6-7.) He will be equally severe with us as with those of the earlier dispensations. The Hebrews of the Christian era were reminded of the fact that "Our God is a consuming fire" (Heb. 12:29). Paul exhorted the Romans, "Behold then the goodness and severity of God: toward them that fell, severity; but toward thee, God's goodness, if thou continue in his goodness; otherwise thou also shalt be cut off" (Rom. 11:22). Here he shows them that if they fail to continue in God's goodness they will become victims of God's severity as was the case with the Jews who rejected God's goodness. The same will be true with us.

When people overlook this unity of Bible revelation and allow their conception of God to be built upon the New Testament alone, it is not surprising that it is distorted and leads to misunderstanding. It must be recognized that the New Testament record is not only closely interlinked with the Old Testament through expressions, illustrations, and quotations which demand an acquaintance with the past to understand, but that it is the last in a progressive series of revelations and is naturally built upon that which had already been made known. Not only had prophecy prepared the way for the coming of the Messiah by declaring in advance much of his life in detail, thus providing unmistakable evidence that Jesus of Nazareth was the one to come, but the historical record of God's dealing with man through a period of some four thousand years abundantly sets forth, in simple objective form, unmistakable manifestation of God's severity as well as his power and his goodness. We should not overlook God's goodness to Abraham and to his decendants through Joseph, the delivery of Israel from Egyptian bondage, the provision of food and guidance through the wilderness, the inheritance in the Land of Canaan, the glory of the kingdom of Solomon, and countless other blessings despite a growing unfaithfulness. Neither should we be unmindful of the destruction of the wicked in the days of Noah, the burning of Sodom and Gomorrah with fire and brimstone, the drowning of the Egyptians in the Red Sea, the thousands of Israel who died of plagues in the wilderness, the annihilation of the nations of Canaan, the Assyrian and Babylonian captivities, and numerous other expressions of God's severity.

If we forget these events of the past, thus neglecting

God's most elemental and most clearly drawn picture of himself, concretely expressed in terms of human activity, and gather our impression from the personal revelation of God through our Lord Jesus Christ, whose life was setting forth the example of self-sacrifice and loving service that man should follow, it is easy to magnify the goodness and loving kindness of God and to minimize or forget his austerity.

It appears that this has happened in varying degrees and with varying effects. The most common effect has been that of emphasizing the teaching on the goodness and blessings of God and slighting or avoiding the teaching on obligations and responsibilities. It has resulted in a gospel that offers the most but requires the least, allowing Christianity to degenerate into a mere form of religion with the major emphasis by some people being upon church membership. Some have been led to teach that in the goodness of God all people will be saved, that even those who have rejected God's pleadings, blasphemed his name, and lived morally disreputable lives will be regenerated in a millennium. Others, forgetful of God's severity as revealed in the Old Testament record, find their conception of God such as forbids their accepting the New Testament teaching that there is a place of eternal punishment for those who know not God.

By these and other related ideas Christianity has been robbed of its seriousness and the force of such New Testament statements as those quoted below has been minimized or neutralized. "A man that hath set at nought Moses' law dieth without compassion on the word of two or three witnesses: of how much sorer punishment, think ye, shall he be judged worthy, who hath trodden under foot the Son of God, and hath counted the blood of the covenant wherewith he was sanctified an unholy thing, and hath done despite unto the Spirit of grace?" (Heb. 10:28-29). "See that ye refuse not him that speaketh. For if they escaped not when they refused him that warned them on earth, much more shall not we escape who turn away from him that warneth from heaven" (Heb. 12:25). "For we know him that said, Vengeance belongeth unto me, I will recompense. And again, The Lord shall judge his people. It is a fearful thing to fall into the hands of the living God" (Heb. 10:30-31). "Let us fear therefore, lest haply, a promise being left of entering into his rest, any one of you should seem to have come short of it" (Heb. 4:1). "Servants, be obedient unto them that according to the flesh are your masters, with fear and trembling, in singleness of your heart, as unto Christ" (Eph. 6:5). "Servants, obey in all things them that are your masters according to the flesh; not with eye-service, as men-pleasers, but in singleness of heart, fearing the Lord" (Col. 3:22). "Well; by their unbelief they were broken off, and thou standest by thy faith. Be not highminded, but fear" (Rom. 11:20). "And if ye call on him as Father, who without respect of persons judgeth according to each man's work, pass the time of your sojourning in fear" (I Pet. 1:17). "But even if ye should suffer for righteousness' sake, blessed are ye: and fear not their fear, neither be troubled; but sanctify in your hearts Christ as Lord: being ready always to give answer to every man that asketh you a reason concerning the hope that is in you, yet with meekness and fear" (I Pet. 3:14-15). "So then, my beloved, even as ye have always obeyed, not as in my presence only, but now much more in my absence, work out your own salvation with fear and trembling" (Phil. 2:12).

The failure to bear in mind the fact that the Bible is the revelation of the one unchanging God has permitted another practice that results in diversity of ideas about Bible teaching without people being aware of the glaring inconsistency involved. Our God is, and was, and ever will be a God of power as well as a God of goodness and of severity. His power has been made known through the accomplishment of things that man could not do—through the working of miracles.

Many people who claim to believe in God want to select some miracles to believe and reject the others, not being aware of the fact that they are rejecting the manifestation of God's power, and at the same time displaying an unbearable inconsistency. How can any person doubt that God is the creator of all things when Paul points to the creation as a manifestation of God's everlasting power and divinity (Rom. 1:20) and the author of Hebrews declares, "By faith we understand that the worlds have been framed by the Word of God, so that what is seen hath not been made out of things which appear" (Heb. 11:3). How can one reject the story of the flood when Jesus said, "And as it came to pass in the days of Noah, even so shall it be also in the days of the Son of man" (Luke 17:26); when the writer of Hebrews tells us that Noah "prepared an ark to the saving of his house; through which he condemned the world, and became heir of the righteousness which is according to faith" (Heb. 11:7); and when the apostle Peter states that God "spared not the ancient world, but preserved Noah with seven others, a preacher of righteousness, when he brought a flood upon the world of the ungodly" (II Pet. 2:5). Why should we question the story of Jonah when the Son of God himself declared to the scribes and Pharisees, "For as Jonah was three days and three nights in the belly of the whale; so shall the Son of man be three days and three nights in the heart of the earth" (Matt. 12:40).

How can we discredit these happenings and accept the New Testament? And again, how can we refuse these and the other miracles of Old Testament days and believe Jesus' miracles recorded in the New Testament? How can we believe that Jesus became the first-born from the dead by the power of God and reject the teaching that he was the first-born of Mary by the power of God through the Holy Spirit? In short, how can we believe in the power of God and yet reject the evidences of God's power?

And how can we doubt that our God has full power over the forces, powers, and conditions of this world and still ascribe to him the power to bring to pass these marvelous changes that lie between us and the kingdom of glory? "Now this I say, brethren, that flesh and blood cannot inherit the kingdom of God; neither doth corruption inherit incorruption. Behold, I tell you a mystery: We all shall not sleep, but we shall all be changed, in a moment, in the twinkling of an eye, at the last trump: for the trumpet shall sound, and the dead shall be raised incorruptible, and we shall be changed. For this corruptible must put on incorruption, and this mortal must put on immortality" (I Cor. 15:50-53).

All of this is to say that we may expect all sorts of variations of Bible interpretations by people who fail to recognize the unity of the Bible and who concoct rationalizations to explain away the parts of the record that do not fit into their own system of thought, even to the undermining of the true concept of the power of God. Any person who would thus blaspheme God's Word by setting aside any part of it as false has repudiated its divinity and given evidence of a mental attitude that disqualifies him as a student of the Bible. If any teacher comes to you confessing that he does not believe part of it, you will do well to be very careful with what he believes about the rest of it.

If we are to understand the Bible we must recognize it to be not only the revelation of the one unchanging God but the one teaching of the God of heaven with the one purpose of bringing man back to God, from whom man through his rejection has become separated. In other words, it not only, through an extended series of historical events, reveals God as one worthy of being enthroned as the ruler of man's heart and life, but teaches man the basic principles of a happy relationship with God. These principles are only statements of the effect upon man that should normally result from God's revelation of himself. The repeated manifestation of his miraculous power through the ages, as recorded in the Old Testament as well as the New Testament, together with his unfailing fulfillment of every promise whether for good or bad, should cause man to believe in him. The repeated demonstration of his goodness and loving kindness should cause man to love and honor him. The unmistakable proof of the severity of his punishment to those who refuse to honor him as God should cause man to fear and reverence him.

To be sure, the principle of faith is the most basic, giving support and meaning to all the rest, but faith can only function in its real strength when it includes all the others. This principle of faith is taught throughout the Bible and unless it becomes operative in man he will never be able to please his creator and consequently will never regain his former place. This fact is tersely expressed in these words, "Without faith it is impossible to be well-pleasing unto him" (Heb. 11:6). Though this statement was made near the close of God's revelation, in the last dispensation, it has been illustrated in God's dealings with man throughout the thousands of years of history and recorded for our admonition.

Not only does the Old Testament record make it

clear that a lack of faith in God always brought man
to grief, but also that by faith man secured for himself
the blessings of the Almighty, regardless of the period
of the world's history in which he lived. It was by faith
that Abel, Enoch, Noah, Abraham, Moses, David,
Samuel, and many others including the prophets received God's blessings. Of this we have a partial sum-
mary in the eleventh chapter of Hebrews.

Not only is faith taught throughout the Bible, but
love has likewise been a part of God's basic teaching to
man. Before the days of Moses our teaching on love as
well as that on faith is by example and not by precept.
There is no record of the people being told to believe
God or to love God. The record simply shows that
when they believed God they obeyed his instruction,
thus showing their love as well as their faith. "This is
the love of God, that ye keep his commandments"
(I John 5:3). From the time of Moses forward, however, the teaching that man should love God and man
is the very heart of their instruction. After quoting
some of the ten commandments of the law, thus showing to which law he referred, Paul declared, "Love
therefore is the fulfillment of the law" (Rom. 13:10).
Since the word *love* is not used in the actual listing of
the ten commandments, its important place in the
teaching might be questioned had we not been given
some very clear and emphatic statements about the
matter. When a certain lawyer asked Jesus, "What
shall I do to inherit eternal life? And he said unto
him, What is written in the law? how readest thou?

And he answering said, Thou shalt love the Lord thy God with all thy heart, and with all thy soul, and with all thy strength, and with all thy mind; and thy neighbor as thyself" (Luke 10:25-27), the lawyer's answer not only shows that the law taught people to love God and man, but also that the lawyer understood the law to teach love for God and man.   On another occasion when Jesus had quoted the same statements quoted by the lawyer he added, "On these two commandments the whole law hangeth, and the prophets" (Matt. 22:40).   In this statement Jesus makes it plain that these two commandments to love God and to love man provide the source and support for all of the individual commandments of the law and all of the work of the prophets as well.   Thus, all of the teaching and work under the law given through Moses was for the purpose of encouraging men to love God and their fellows.

We now come to the question, "How has this basic teaching on faith and love led people to be at variance on Bible interpretation?"   It is through the relative evaluation that has been given to the basic teaching in comparison with that given to the concrete practices of man's living, through the importance placed upon the Bible teaching on faith and love and that assigned to the individual acts through which man expresses his faith and love.

Faith and love are words that name or describe attitudes or sentiments within man with regard to things or persons about him, including God.   Man's practices or ways of doing are expressions of his attitudes or

sentiments. Since God made man as well as all the
other objects of creation, and also the laws which con-
trol them all, he certainly should occupy the place of
greatest influence over man's attitudes and sentiments.
This he expects to do. He reveals himself as worthy
of this place and teaches man through examples and
precepts that it will be for man's own good and happiness to believe in God implicitly and love him with all
his being. A genuine faith in God is an attitude toward
God of unquestioned confidence in the truth of his
revelation and the wisdom of his instruction, and an
unwavering assurance of his promises to those who
accept his wisdom. A true love for God (as man is
taught to love God with all his heart, etc.) which will
naturally result from such a faith is an attitude that
seeks a way to express itself. Not only so, but it seeks
the way that will please the one who is loved. The
man who loves his wife will seek to do the things she
wants him to do and also in the way she wants them
done. So it is with the man who loves God. He will
earnestly seek to do what God wants him to do and
to do it as God wants it done. Thus, one who really
believes in God and loves him (unless he is misguided)
wants to know the practices he can follow day by day
to best show his love for God, and in no case would he
consider the wish (or commandment) of God unimpor-
tant, especially since God has shown that this is the
real substance of love. "For this is the love of God, that
we keep his commandments" (I John 5:3).

Now with these thoughts before us, we are ready for

a more complete answer to our question. Some people have apparently considered faith and love attitudes complete within their mental sphere and fully pleasing to God without any expression of themselves in ways of living or acting. These, of course, emphasize the teaching on faith and love as more or less abstract things with no particular practical significance, thus making them and the religions which they support purely theoretical. Other people feel that man should do something to show his faith and love but that it can be done according to his own idea, or at least with full liberty in the matter. They stress the basic teachings of the Bible but minimize the need for following specific practices in full keeping with the Book. Still others accept the Bible teaching on faith and love as portraying actual vital principles of life that must be lived and lived according to God's instructions or wishes. These seek to make faith and love living principles that demand diligence in seeking to know and do the will of God from the heart. There are still others who appear to have lost sight of the vital relationship between faith and love, and doing the things that God would have us do in the way that God would have us do them. In their fear that men will be led to neglect the careful practice of those things through which they must show their faith and love (knowing that some have been so led) they minimize the teaching on love especially and stress the doing of some of the things, that the man who loves God will do. In doing this the impression is given that man today is serving God under a law of works apart from the principles through which the works must be motivated. At times, their misplaced emphasis gives the impression that they are dealing with the law of Christ in a way similar to the way the scribes and Pharisees dealt with the law of Moses whom Jesus warned, "Woe unto you, scribes and Pharisees, hypocrites! for ye tithe mint and anise and cummin, and have left undone the weightier matters of the law, justice, and mercy, and faith: but these ye ought to have done, and not to have left the other undone" (Matt. 23:23).

There are also a few people of the last group mentioned whose reaction against some who do not join them in their over-emphasis of teaching on works to the neglect of the principle of love, who appear to be causing further confusion by misusing the word "love." They use it as a term to indicate "softness" or "doing somewhat as one pleases," while a proper understanding of love as a principle of Christianity connotes more strict demands of people than did the law of Moses, rather than a carelessness and a looseness.

As we leave this topic, we should not forget that the Bible is the revelation of one unchanging God and its basic requirement of men of all generations is a faith in God that works through love. It has taught men of different periods to do different things in expressing their love for God. Differences in Bible interpretations have arisen from different conceptions of God and by unbalanced emphasis on either the basic teaching of the Bible or its detailed teaching.

QUESTIONS ON LECTURE X

1. To properly understand God's teaching how must the Bible be viewed?
2. How was this illustrated from the field of music?
3. What is the first thing that should be borne in mind by one who would understand the Bible?
4. Show that God was equally good and equally severe with the Jews as with us.
5. What is the danger in allowing one's conception of God to be built upon the New Testament teaching only?
6. State some apparent effects of such a narrowed conception of God.
7. Use some statements which indicate the true seriousness of Christian living.
8. Show the inconsistency in refusing to believe some of the miracles recorded in the Bible and retaining a hope in eternal life.
9. What warning is given in regard to the teacher who confesses that he does not believe part of the Bible?
10. What are the basic teachings of the whole Bible?
11. Why is the principle of faith the most basic?
12. Show that love is the very heart of the instruction under the law of Moses.
13. State how the teaching on faith and love has given rise to many differences in Bible interpretation.
14. What word is sometimes misued to indicate softness?
15. What causes of differences in Bible interpretation are given in this lecture?

THE BIBLE ORGANIZATION

A T this time we shall study the organization of the Bible as it relates to understanding Bible teaching. Some of the differences arising from failure to recognize the unity in Bible revelation and from variation of emphasis given to the basic teaching of the Bible have already been pointed out. We shall now turn our attention to the individualization of teaching to the people of the respective dispensations.

Even though there is complete harmony throughout the Bible on its basic teaching, there is some diversity in the teachings given to men in different periods of Bible history. In other words, faith and love are principles taught to all generations and are absolutely necessary to all, but the detailed practices through which man expresses his faith and love do not continue to be the same. God has not taught Abraham or Moses to do what he has taught us to do today; neither has he taught us to do all that Abraham or Moses did.

As has already been mentioned, God's revelation of himself is progressive in nature, coming to its fullness in the Lord Jesus Christ who declared, "He that hath seen me hath seen the Father" (John 14:9). Likewise, his teaching is developmental in nature, growing, expanding, and changing with the passing of generations, keeping pace with the increasing revelation of God until "the perfect law, the law of liberty" was given through the only begotten Son of God. Since this is true, it is imperative that we survey the teachings of God in their developmental relationships if we are to understand the background of some very marked religious differences. With this purpose in mind, we shall now review the Bible organization.

We shall begin this review with a brief outline of the Bible record. Since it is a historical record of God's dealings with man as well as a record of God's teaching to man, and since God's teaching to man has always been concerned with and, in fact, determined by man's relationship to God, it appears that the most natural and most meaningful outline should set forth man's history in terms of his relationship to God.

I. Man's origin and close association with God (Gen. 1-3).
II. The long period of man's estrangement from God (Gen. 4 through Mal.).
    A. Man's sinfulness and destruction by water (Gen. 4-8).
    B. Man in the new world until Abraham (Gen. 9-11).
    C. God's promise to Abraham and adoption of the Jewish people (Gen. 12-50).
    D. The sinfulness of the Jews and the law of Moses (Exod. 1 through Mal. 4).
III. The period of man's reconciliation to God (Matt. through Rev.).
    A. The days of preparation (Matt. through John).
    B. Man's blessings in Christ through the promise to Abraham (Acts through Rev.).

With this outline before us, let us now make further examination of the organization of the book that we may see the relationship between the parts and be better qualified to understand its teaching and to discover some of the sources of religious differences. As we continue, we should bear in mind the three main divisions of man's history. Man began his existence in close association with his Maker in a wonderful garden unmarred by the ravages of sin. When man ceased to give God the honor and turned his efforts toward seeking honor for himself, he thereby broke the sacred relationship and, according to the information that had already been given to him, he was immediately separated from God. Thus began the long period of man's estrangement from God. This estrangement continued through a period of approximately four thousand years, during which time God made further preparation for the fuller revelation of himself and in the fulness of time Jesus came, revealing him to the world and also becoming the propitiation for man's sin. Paul tells us, "That God was in Christ reconciling the world unto himself" (II Cor. 5:19). So the final atonement for sin and the real reconciliation of man to God came through the Lord Jesus Christ, through whom many people have been led to turn away from themselves, showing by their faith and loving service that they have been reconciled to God, and to await the promise of the great day of restoration when they may return to him in glory.

Now with this picture in mind let us make a closer inspection of the Bible record itself. In the record of man's origin and close association with God we are told but little.   We are given a short statement of the creation, including man, an implication of man's peace and happiness, a graphic picture of the termination of this association by a single act of disobedience on the part of man, and a prophetic statement of man's work and struggle with sin.   The only instruction given to man was that which concerned his general physical progress and that which related to life in that special environment.   Thus, no occasion is given in this part of the Bible record for differences in religious teaching or practice.

The record of the first part of the long period of man's estrangement from God so far as we are concerned is fully historical, giving us man's genealogy from Adam to Noah, something of the righteousness of Abel and Enoch, a description of man's exceeding sinfulness, a record of man's destruction by water and the salvation of Noah and his family.   There is no record of any instruction to man except that directly concerning the ark and the flood.   So this part of the Bible record provides no occasion for differences in Bible teaching or practice.

In the second part of the long period of man's estrangement from God we find Noah, the preacher of righteousness, and his family in a new world with the privilege of making a new start.   Our record of this period of some three hundred and fifty years to the time of Abraham is also very scant.   It tells us of Noah's offering a sacrifice unto Jehovah, of his planting a vineyard and becoming drunk from the wine thereof, of the curse of Canaan, of the descendents of Noah, and of God's covenant not to destroy the world again by water. Noah and his sons were urged to be fruitful and multiply and the only other instruction given to them was that the blood of animals was not to be eaten and, "Whoso sheddeth man's blood, by man shall his blood be shed: for in the image of God made he man" (Gen. 9:6). Since the question of eating the blood of animals has been given practically no attention in our religious life, and since the practice of taking the life of a man as a punishment for his shedding the blood of his fellow man has been generally accepted in our social system, we find no teachings during these days of Noah that serve as a basis for religious differences today. We are given practically no information in regard to the descendents of Noah prior to the days of Abraham. There is indication in the statement made by Laban at the time of his and Jacob's separation that Abraham's family, including his father before him, were worshipers of God, "The God of Abraham, and the God of Nahor, the God of their father, judge betwixt us" (Gen. 31:53).

The record of the third part of man's long period of estrangement from God tells us of God's calling Abram out of his country and from his people and of the promises of God to him. It tells how Abram by faith left the land of his birth, went into the land of Canaan, served God for a period of approximately ten years, worshiping him at the altar from place to place as he had evidently been instructed. It tells of God appearing unto Abraham in a vision and declaring unto him that the promise made unto him should be fulfilled through seed from his own loins; it tells that Abram believed God, despite the ten years of waiting and the idea which he had conceived that the promise would be fulfilled through one of his household, and that this faith was reckoned unto Abram for righteousness. Also the record reveals that fourteen years later, after the affair with Hagar, when God was about to make known unto Abram that Sarai would be the mother of his promised seed, that God gave to Abraham the covenant of circumcision for an everlasting covenant and declared unto him, "And the uncircumcised male who is not circumcised in the flesh of his foreskin, that soul shall be cut off from his people; he hath broken my covenant" (Gen. 17:14).

We learn also of how Abraham continued in this faith, even to the offering of Isaac upon the altar, at which time the promise to him was reiterated with an oath, "And the angel of Jehovah called unto Abraham a second time out of heaven, and said, By myself have I sworn, saith Jehovah, because thou hast done this thing, and hast not withheld thy son, thine only son, that in blessing I will bless thee, and in multiplying I will multiply thy seed as the stars of the heavens, and as the sand which is upon the seashore; and thy seed shall possess the gate of his enemies; and in thy seed shall all the nations of the earth be blessed; because thou hast obeyed my voice" (Gen. 22:15-18). In this restatement of the promise, we have a definite reason for the promise being given unto Abraham, "And in thy seed shall all the nations of the earth be blessed: because thou hast obeyed my voice." With the exception of the instruction given to Abraham, "Walk before me, and be thou perfect" (Gen. 17:1), all of the remainder of the teaching in the record of this period from the time that God called Abraham out of the land of his nativity unto the time when Joseph was embalmed and put into the coffin in Egypt is personal in character. In fact, there is but one item of instruction in this record that could give rise to religious differences and that is the teaching of circumcision. But circumcision seems to have never been made an issue among the religious people who propose to accept the Bible as the Word of God.

There are two important factors that should be called to mind that are very helpful in understanding the next section of the Bible record. The first is the fact that this promise made to Abraham is the basis of all of our hopes through Christ. This, Paul makes unmistakably clear in his letter to the Galatian people. "And the scripture, foreseeing that God would justify the Gentiles by faith, preached the gospel beforehand unto Abraham, saying, In thee shall all the nations be blessed" (Gal. 3:8). "Now to Abraham were the promises spoken, and to his seed. He saith not, And to seeds, as of many; but as of one, And to thy seed, which is Christ. Now this I say: A covenant confirmed beforehand by God, the law, which came four hundred and thirty years after, doth not disannul, so as to make the promise of none effect. For if the inheritance is of the law, it is no more of promise: but God hath granted it to Abraham by promise" (Gal. 3:16-18). "Christ redeemed us from the curse of the law, having become a curse for us; for it is written, Cursed is every one that hangeth on a tree: that upon the Gentiles might come the blessing of Abraham in Christ Jesus; that we might receive the promise of the Spirit through faith" (Gal. 3:13-14). "And if ye are Christ's, then are ye Abraham's seed, heirs according to promise" (Gal. 3:29). "Now we, brethren, as Isaac was, are children of promise" (Gal. 4:28).

The second fact is that the descendents of Abraham through the sons of Jacob did not continue to walk in the steps of the faith of Abraham. It seems that we have been made fully aware of the fact that, "There arose a new king over Egypt, who knew not Joseph" (Exod. 1:8), but have given little attention to the fact that there had arisen in Egypt a people, Israel, descendents of the sons of Jacob, who knew not God. Of this, Ezekiel reminded the children of Israel. "But they rebelled against me, and would not hearken unto me; they did not every man cast away the abominations of their eyes, neither did they forsake the idols of Egypt. Then I said I would pour out my wrath upon them, to accomplish my anger against them in the midst of the land of Egypt" (Ezek. 20:8). Not long before Moses' death he declared unto the children of Israel, "Ye have been rebellious against Jehovah from the day that I knew you" (Deut. 9:24). God did not deliver the people from Egyptian bondage because of their righteousness or their love for him but because of his covenant with Abraham. "And God heard their groaning, and God remembered his covenant with Abraham, with Isaac, and with Jacob" (Exod. 2:24).

In these two great contrasting factors—the great promises of God to the Jewish people, and their continued rebellion against him—we have depicted the terrible ugliness of the last period of man's estrangement from God. The record of this period furnishes us the history of this rebellious people, together with the law through which God controlled them and of which Paul declared that in it was the form of knowledge and of the truth (Rom. 2:20). Paul also tells us that, "It was added because of transgressions, till the seed should come to whom the promise hath been made" (Gal. 3:19). And also, "But before faith came, we were kept in ward under the law, shut up unto the faith which should afterwards be revealed. So that the law is become our tutor to bring us unto Christ, that we might be justified by faith" (Gal. 3:23-24). Here we have a statement of the cause, the purpose, and the temporary nature of the law. "Added because of transgression," "kept in ward under the law," "to bring us unto Christ," and to remain in force "till the seed should come," and since he had come they were "no longer under a tutor."

The law was a law of restraint and of instruction. It was not a law of salvation. This Paul makes clear in the following statements. "Because by the works of the law shall no flesh be justified in his sight; for through the law cometh the knowledge of sin" (Rom. 3:20). "Now that no man is justified by the law before God, is evident: for, The righteous shall live by faith; and the law is not of faith; but, He that doeth them shall live in them" (Gal. 3:11-12). "We being Jews by nature, and not sinners of the Gentiles, yet knowing that a man is not justified by the works of the law but through faith in Jesus Christ, even we believed on Christ Jesus, that we might be justified by faith in Christ, and not by the works of the law: because by the works of the law shall no flesh be justified" (Gal. 2: 15-16). "I do not make void the grace of God: for if righteousness is through the law, then Christ died for nought" (Gal. 2:21).

From these statements we find that the sinfulness of these people was to be made known to them through the law; that the law was not of faith, for these people had turned away from the faith of their father Abraham, being a rebellious people. So they were shut up under the law that they might be brought to faith through the fuller revelation of God in the Lord Jesus Christ. They had failed to become an heir of the righteousness which is according to faith as did Noah. "By faith Noah, being warned of God concerning things not seen as yet, moved with godly fear, prepared an ark to the saving of his house; through which he condemned the world, and became heir of the righteousness which is according to faith" (Heb. 11:7). For the righteous must live by faith. Paul gives further emphasis to this in a description of the case of Abraham,

"To Abraham his faith was reckoned for righteousness. How then was it reckoned? when he was in circumcision, or in uncircumcision? Not in circumcision, but in uncircumcision: and he received the sign of circumcision, a seal of the righteousness of the faith which he had while he was in uncircumcision: that he might be the father of all them that believe, though they be in uncircumcision, that righteousness might be reckoned unto them; and the father of circumcision to them who not only are of the circumcision, but who also walk in the steps of that faith of our father Abraham which he had in uncircumcision. For not through the law was the promise to Abraham or to his seed that he should be heir of the world, but through the righteousness of faith. For if they that are of the law are heirs, faith is made void, and the promise is made of none effect" (Rom. 4:9-14). This statement also indicates why the majority of the Jews failed. They depended upon the form of the law, being rebellious, and having failed to walk in the steps of that faith which was in Abraham. And being merely of the law, and not of faith, they were not heirs of righteousness.

Furthermore, Paul makes it clear that those who have received Christ, even those that were under the law, are no longer obligated to the teachings of the law, "For ye are not under the law, but under grace" (Rom. 6:14). "Ye also were made dead to the law through the body of Christ" (Rom. 7:4). "But now we have been discharged from the law, having died to that wherein we were held; so that we serve in newness of the spirit, and not in oldness of the letter" (Rom. 7:6). "For Christ is the end of the law unto righteousness to every one that believeth" (Rom. 10:4). And speaking of himself, who was a Jew, Paul said, "For I through the law died unto the law, that I might live unto God" (Gal. 2:19). In speaking of Christ to the Ephesians, Paul said, "For he is our peace, who made both one, and brake down the middle wall of partition, having abolished in his flesh the enmity, even the law of commandments contained in ordinances" (Eph. 2:14-15). And to the Colossians he said, "Having blotted out the bond written in ordinances that was against us, which was contrary to us: and he hath taken it out of the way, nailing it to the cross" (Col. 2:14). In preaching Christ to the people on Solomon's porch, Peter told them, "Moses indeed said, A prophet shall the Lord God raise up unto you from among your brethren, like unto me; to him shall ye hearken in all things whatsoever he shall speak unto you. And it shall be, that every soul that shall not hearken to that prophet, shall be utterly destroyed from among the people" (Acts 3:22-23). And Paul on another occasion warned against the grave danger of turning away from faith in Christ to place any dependence upon the teaching of the law. "Behold, I Paul say unto you, that, if ye receive circumcision, Christ will profit you nothing. Yea, I testify again to every man that receiveth circumcision, that he is a debtor to do the whole law. Ye are severed from Christ, ye who would be justified by the law; ye are fallen away from grace" (Gal. 5:2-4).

After reading these plain statements, and many others of this same nature in the New Testament teaching about the law, some say that all of these refer to the ceremonial law and that certainly the ceremonial law with its Levitical system has been taken out of the way, but that the ten commandments which were written upon the tables of stone by the finger of God still remain and that we are subject to every one of them just as those people were who were led out of the land of Egypt. Now on this, I would not be misunderstood. As has been said before, the basic teachings of faith in God and love for God and man have always been a part of God's teaching and ever will be. Not, however, because they are expressed in the law, but because they are taught throughout the Bible and are exemplified in the life of the Lord Jesus Christ, being the very heart of his teaching. However, the ten commandments as a part of the law given through Moses on Mount Sinai have been taken out of the way.

But now let us turn to the Bible teaching for unmistakable evidence that this is the truth. Since there is a quibble over the use of the term "law," we shall seek our evidence in those statements which use other terms about which there can be no quibble. We now turn to the Hebrew letter which was evidently addressed particularly to those who at one time were under the law. "But now hath he obtained a ministry the more excellent, by so much as he is also the mediator of a better covenant, which hath been enacted upon better promises. For if that first covenant had

been faultless, then would no place have been sought
for a second" (Heb. 8:6-7). Our word here, of course,
is the word *covenant*. Jesus brought a better covenant
because the first was not faultless. It was not because
Jehovah needed to make a second try to make a faultless covenant, but because of the nature of the people,
it was only a temporary covenant. Now to be sure
that the writer has reference to the covenant made at
Mount Sinai, we read, "For finding fault with them, he
saith, Behold, the days come, saith the Lord, That I
will make a new covenant with the house of Israel and
with the house of Judah; not according to the covenant
that I made with their fathers in the day that I took
them by the hand to lead them forth out of the land
of Egypt; For they continued not in my covenant, And
I regarded them not, saith the Lord" (Heb. 8:8-9).
And further evidence of this fact is found in the following statement. "Wherefore even the first covenant hath
not been dedicated without blood. For when every
commandment had been spoken by Moses unto all the
people according to the law, he took the blood of the
calves and the goats, with water and scarlet wool and
hyssop, and sprinkled both the book itself and all the
people, saying, This is the blood of the covenant which
God commanded to you-ward" (Heb. 9:18-20). The
record of the happening referred to here is found in
Exodus, chapter 24, verses 7 and 8, and happened at
Mount Sinai when the covenant or law was given.
Referring to the covenant again, the writer declares,

"He taketh away the first, that he may establish the second" (Heb. 10:9).

Having seen that the first covenant has been taken away and that Christ has become a mediator of a better covenant, we turn now to Moses' writings recorded in Deuteronomy for the unmistakable identification of the word "covenant" with the ten commandments. "And it came to pass at the end of forty days and forty nights, that Jehovah gave me the two tables of stone, even the tables of the covenant" (Deut. 9:11). "And I turned and came down from the mount, and put the tables in the ark which I had made; and there they are as Jehovah commanded me" (Deut. 10:5). "And he declared unto you his covenant, which he commanded you to perform, even the ten commandments; and he wrote them upon two tables of stone. And Jehovah commanded me at that time to teach you statutes and ordinances, that ye might do them in the land whither ye go over to possess it. Take ye therefore good heed unto yourselves; for ye saw no manner of form on the day that Jehovah spake unto you in Horeb out of the midst of the fire" (Deut. 4:13-15). If these statements be true, and certainly they are, the first covenant which Jesus has taken out of the way included the ten commandments. The reason for saying, "included the ten commandments," there was much else given in the covenant on Mount Sinai which Moses wrote into a book and is referred to as the "book of the covenant" (Exod. 24:7).

For some reason, people have been inclined to exalt

the ten commandments and practically overlook the relationship between them and the Levitical priesthood, while the fact is, they were given to support the priesthood and to serve as a guide for the people as they worshiped God under the Levitical priesthood. Hence, the writer of the book of Hebrews reasons from this fact in his effort to show the Jews that the covenant or the law has been changed. "Now if there was perfection through the Levitical priesthood (for under it hath the people received the law), what further need was there that another priest should arise after the order of Melchizedek, and not be reckoned after the order of Aaron?" (Heb. 7:11). When Jesus, who was of the tribe of Judah (Heb. 7:14) became high priest after the order of Melchizedek (he was not of the tribe of Levi and therefore could not be high priest under the Levitical priesthood) there was a change in the priesthood. In other words, the Levitical priesthood was discontinued so the law given under it was changed. "For the priesthood being changed, there is made of necessity a change also of the law" (Heb. 7:12). When the Levites were priests, the law given through Moses was in force. When Jesus became high priest, the law of Christ supplanted the law of Moses, the basic teachings of both being the same.

It is indeed strange that the one commandment of the ten that is the most closely related to the Levitical priesthood and the Jewish system of feasts is the one that many people insist upon including with the teachings of Christ. This is the fourth commandment, "Remember the sabbath day, to keep it holy" (Exod. 20:8). Some only apply it in a figure to the first day of the week, the Lord's day, commonly known to us as Sunday, by quoting it in an effort to impress the urgency of worship under the Christian teaching, while others insist upon its literal application relative to the day of worship. Since it has been shown that this commandment, together with the other nine, has been taken away, and since the New Testament nowhere indicates or implies in any way that it is a part of the teaching of Christ, it is sometimes suggested that it was a teaching given to man even before the law. We should recall that the teachings given during the early periods of man's history, up until the time of Moses, have been carefully checked and not one word of instruction to keep the sabbath was found in the record and not one occasion of its being kept. The record of the first instruction to man in regard to keeping the sabbath and also the first observance of the sabbath is found in the sixteenth chapter of the book of Exodus. On that occasion in the wilderness of Sin which God began to feed his people manna from heaven, we are told in the fourth verse of that chapter that it was used at this time to prove the people whether they would walk in God's law. "Then said Jehovah unto Moses, Behold, I will rain bread from heaven for you; and the people shall go out and gather a day's portion every day, that I may prove them, whether they will walk in my law, or not" (Exod. 16:4). Nehemiah speaks of the sabbath being made known to the people when the law was given from Sinai. "Thou camest down also upon mount Sinai, and spakest with them from heaven, and gavest them right ordinances and true laws, good statutes and commandments, and madest known unto them thy holy sabbath, and commandest them commandments, and statutes, and a law, by Moses thy servant" (Neh. 9: 13-14). Moses gives the reason for God's command to keep the sabbath in these words, "And thou shalt remember that thou wast a servant in the land of Egypt, and Jehovah thy God brought thee out thence by a mighty hand and by an outstretched arm: therefore Jehovah thy God commanded thee to keep the sabbath day" (Deut. 5:15). In view of the facts stated in the verses quoted, it appears evident that the teaching to keep the sabbath was given only to the people who were brought out of the land of Egypt and their descendents as a part of the law.

However, since in the record in Exodus, chapter 20, verse 11, in connection with the teaching of the fourth commandment, reference is made to the fact that the creation was in six days and that God rested on the seventh day, some people might accept this as implying that this hallowed day had been observed down through the generations. For the purpose of studying the matter further, suppose we granted that such might have been the case. Then what? Would that necessarily indicate that the teaching was to continue after the law had been nullified.

For the sake of comparison, let us now consider a teaching that did actually exist before the giving of the law and was practiced that became a definite part of the Jewish teaching in connection with the law, and see what became of it. The teaching referred to is the teaching on circumcision. We have already learned that circumcision was given unto Abraham as a token of the covenant of promise and was strictly required of the people of Israel before they could participate in the first passover that was eaten in the land of Egypt (Exod. 12:48) and continued to be a part of the Jewish system under the Levitical priesthood. What about the practice of circumcision as a religious rite among those who had accepted the teachings of Christ? Paul makes it clear that it was no longer required but as such was forbidden. "Yea, I testify again to every man that receiveth circumcision, that he is a debtor to do the whole law. Ye are severed from Christ, ye who would be justified by the law; ye are fallen away from grace" (Gal. 5:3-4). This being the case in regard to the teaching on circumcision, which we know to have been a very definite part of God's teaching before the giving of the law, why should we suppose that keeping the sabbath should continue as a practice of Christian people when it was an expressed part of the covenant which the Saviour took out of the way and of which we have no definite record that it was a part of any teaching prior to the law?

We have made some examination of the Bible teaching in regard to the sabbath because this question has been the basis, and is yet, of some of our most marked differences, and also to illustrate how differences arise when people ignore the organization of the Bible and thus fail to understand the relationships that exist. We should not forget that the Bible is a record of progressive revelation and developmental teaching, retaining the basic principles throughout but varying in the teaching of specific practices from dispensation to dispensation. We should remember further that there are no specific teachings recorded before the time of Moses over which serious differences in interpretation could arise. And we should be conscious of the fact that when we propose to supplement God's teaching through the Lord Jesus Christ by teachings that were given through Moses, we are unwilling to put our trust in that teaching which God sent for man's reconciliation, but prefer to place our confidence, at least in part, in that teaching which God sent to restrain a rebellious people and to point them to the teachings of reconciliation. We should not overlook the fact that such a practice humiliates the Son of God and exalts Moses.

QUESTIONS ON LECTURE XI

1. What Bible teachings have remained the same but what has changed from one dispensation to another?
2. The most natural and most meaningful outline of the Bible should be expressed in terms of what?
3. Describe the three major periods of the Bible history of man as given in the three main divisions of the outline.
4. What is the nature of the teaching given in the record of the first period of man's history?
5. Why have no religious divisions been caused by the teaching during man's sinfulness and destruction by water?

6. State the only direct teachings given in the Bible record between the flood and the call of Abraham.

7. Have either of these teachings become the source of religious differences?

8. What is the only teaching given to Abraham or to the Jews as a family that could give rise to religious differences?

9. Why was the promise to bless all nations through the seed of Abraham made sure unto him?

10. State two important facts that are helpful in understanding the Jewish history from the time of Moses forward.

11. Give evidence to support each of these facts.

12. Why was the law of Moses given and what purpose was it to serve?

13. Give evidence that it was a law of restraint and not a law of salvation.

14. In what had the people under the law of Moses already failed? Explain fully.

15. Give evidence that the Jews who received the teachings of Christ were no longer under the law.

16. Give Moses' statement as quoted by Peter which shows that Moses knew that this was to come to pass.

17. What did Paul say of the status of Christians who received circumcision?

18. Show clearly that the Ten Commandments were a part of the law that was taken out of the way.

19. What was the change in the priesthood that made the change in law necessary?

20. Which one of the Ten Commandments was most closely related to the Levitical priesthood and the Jewish system of feasts?

21. State two ways that people attempt to make it a part of our present teaching.

22. Do we have any record where a man was taught to keep the sabbath before the people of Israel were brought out of Egyptian bondage?

23. Where is the record of the first teaching to keep the Sabbath and under what condition was it given?

24. Where did Nehemiah say the holy Sabbath was made known to Israel?

25. What reason did Moses give to the people for keeping the Sabbath?

26. What statement is made in connection with the giving of the fourth commandment that some people have taken to imply that the Sabbath had been observed down through the ages?

27. Were we to grant that this is correct, give reasoning to show that Sabbath observance was taken away with the rest of the law?

28. What does our effort to supplement God's teaching through Christ by earlier teaching through Moses indicate?

29. In reality what is being done when we do this?

ORGANIZATION AND NATURE OF THE NEW TESTAMENT

WE have given consideration to the nature and general organization of the Bible, have examined the relationship which exists between the teachings of the respective dispensations, and have learned that, "God, having of old time spoken unto the fathers in the prophets by divers portions and in divers manners, hath at the end of these days spoken unto us in his Son, whom he appointed heir of all things, through whom also he made the worlds" (Heb. 1:1-2). The people of earlier days were to hear Moses and the prophets, but after those days those who would be reconciled to God were to hear his Son. He brought the ministry of reconciliation to which God bore testimony on the mount of transfiguration when Moses and Elijah appeared with Jesus before Peter, James and John. Peter suggested that they build there three tabernacles, one for Jesus, one for Moses, and one for Elijah. "While he was yet speaking, behold, a bright cloud overshadowed them: and behold, a voice out of the cloud, saying, This is my beloved Son, in whom I am well pleased; hear ye him" (Matt. 17:5). Certainly there is but one meaining that can be assigned to this testimony given under these conditions, and that is that the time of hearing Moses and the time of hearing Elijah

177

was past. From this time forward, they should hear the
only begotten Son of God. When Peter was preaching
about Jesus to the people gathered in Solomon's porch,
he would have them understand that Moses knew that
the time would come for them to hear another. "Moses
indeed said, A prophet shall the Lord God raise up
unto you from among your brethren, like unto me; to
him shall ye hearken in all things whatsoever he shall
speak unto you. And it shall be, that every soul that
shall not hearken to that prophet, shall be utterly
destroyed from among the people" (Acts 3:22-23). If
we are to hear this prophet, Jesus, in all things, this
excludes our going back to the Old Testament teaching
for any teaching or doctrine in anywise contrary to, or
not included in, the teachings of Jesus himself. Those
teachings were not given to us. We were never under
the old covenant. Why should we reflect upon the
new covenant by reverting to the old in an effort to
establish some practice to be followed by God's people
today? This is exactly what Paul was teaching the
Galatian people against in his letter addressed to them.
What did he say? "I marvel that ye are so quickly
removing from him that called you in the grace of
Christ unto a different gospel; which is not another
gospel: only there are some that trouble you, and would
pervert the gospel of Christ. But though we, or an
angel from heaven, should preach unto you any gospel
other than that which we preached unto you, let him
be anathema. As we have said before, so say I now
again, If any man preacheth unto you any gospel other

than that which ye received, let him be anathema" (Gal. 1:6-9).

The third natural division of the Bible, the period of man's reconciliation, further naturally divides into two parts: the period of preparation, and the final fulfillment of the promise to Abraham through Jesus Christ as his seed. Part one of the third division, the period of preparation (Matthew, Mark, Luke and John), has for its purpose the establishment of the fact that Jesus of Nazareth is the Son of God and the seed of Abraham through whom all the nations were to be blessed. The evidences were provided through John the Baptist and his work and the work of Jesus himself. The message of the two was basically the same, "Repent ye; for the kingdom of heaven is at hand" (Matt. 3:2; 4:17).

John states his part in this period of preparation as follows, "And I knew him not; but that he should be made manifest to Israel, for this cause came I baptizing in water. And John bare witness, saying, I have beheld the Spirit descending as a dove out of heaven; and it abode upon him. And I knew him not: but he that sent me to baptize in water, he said unto me, Upon whomsoever thou shalt see the Spirit descending, and abiding upon him, the same is he that baptizeth in the Holy Spirit. And I have seen, and have borne witness that this is the Son of God" (John 1:31-34). It was his work to bring many of the Jews to repentance, to turn their hearts toward the Messiah, to gain a place of respect and leadership that he might receive the sign and bear witness to the fact that Jesus of Nazareth was the Son of God. In accomplishing his work, John taught many lessons on repentance and right living. John showed the relationship that existed between him and Jesus and between them and the church when he referred to Christ saying, "He that hath the bride is the bridegroom" (John 3:29), and described himself as the friend of the bridegroom. Further recognition of the temporary nature of his work was shown when he referred to Christ saying, "He must increase, but I must decrease" (John 3:30).

Jesus fulfilled the prophecies of the past and made and fulfilled many others. He performed miracles above number, he exemplified the principles of his teaching and trained the twelve for bearing witness of him, after he had provided the unmistakable evidences of his divinity through his death, burial and resurrection. He set things in final readiness after his resurrection from the dead, at which time he commissioned the twelve to reveal God's love to the world by preaching "Christ crucified" and charged them to wait in Jerusalem until they received power from on high.

The second part of the period of man's reconciliation to God—man's blessings in Christ through the promise to Abraham (Acts of the Apostles, the Epistles and Revelation)—makes known the establishment of the kingdom of God and the good tidings of eternal salvation in Christ, the seed of Abraham. This statement is supported by the following facts.

The blessings promised to Abraham were to be to all the nations. "And in thy seed shall all the nations of the earth be blessed; because thou hast obeyed my voice" (Gen. 22:18). The crucifixion was necessary before the blessings of Abraham could come upon the Gentiles (all nations except Jews). "Christ redeemed us from the curse of the law, having become a curse for us; for it is written, Cursed is every one that hangeth on a tree: that upon the Gentiles might come the blessing of Abraham in Christ Jesus; that we might receive the promise of the Spirit through faith" (Gal. 3:13-14). Peter showed that David knew that the kingdom would not be established until after the resurrection. "Being therefore a prophet, and knowing that God had sworn with an oath to him, that of the fruit of his loins he would set one upon his throne; he foreseeing this spake of the resurrection of the Christ" (Acts 2:30-31). The kingdom had not been established at the time of the ascension. "They therefore, when they were come together, asked him, saying, Lord, dost thou at this time restore the kingdom to Israel?" (Acts 1:6). The kingdom had been established when Peter was speaking on the first Pentecost after the ascension, for he urged, "Let all the house of Israel therefore know assuredly, that God hath made him both Lord and Christ, this Jesus whom ye crucified" (Acts 2:36). Peter also declared, "Being therefore by the right hand of God exalted, and having received of the Father the promise of the Holy Spirit, he hath poured forth this, which ye see and hear" (Acts 2:33). Here Peter was telling what had happened that morning of which the record says, "And they were all filled with the Holy

Spirit, and began to speak with other tongues, as the Spirit gave them utterance" (Acts 2:4). Thus began the actual fulfillment of the promise made to Abraham when the good tidings of the establishment of the kingdom began to be announced to the Jews that were "from every nation under heaven" (Acts 2:5), and shortly thereafter to the Gentiles of these nations.

The book of Acts also gives us a bit of the history of the apostles and their personal proclamation of the principles of reconciliation. The epistles provide us with a further delineation of the principles of reconciliation and instruction to those who had accepted reconciliation. The book of Revelation gives further emphasis to the same principles through a symbolic presentation.

One of the principal sources of religious differences in this part of the Bible record is the failure to recognize the relationship between the period of preparation and the true period of reconciliation. This failure and the influence of some of the human weaknesses (ignorance, deception, conceit) have led many people to give a higher evaluation to some of Jesus' personal statements than they have given to his teaching through the apostles guided by the Holy Spirit. To be sure, the personal teachings of Jesus are important. They are the Word of God and should be treated as such. However, in our dealing with his personal statements made to individuals, we must not overlook the conditions under which they were made if we are to understand them. For example, if the words, "Fear not, only believe," had been used in answering the question, "What must I do to be saved?" the meaning would be quite different from what it is as they are used. They were never used in answer to such a question, but were spoken by Jesus to Jairus who had besought Jesus to come to heal his little daughter who was at the point of death. But before Jesus and Jairus reached the house, "They come from the ruler of the synagogue's house, saying, Thy daughter is dead: why troublest thou the Teacher any further? But Jesus, not heeding the word spoken, saith unto the ruler of the synagogue, Fear not, only believe" (Mark 5:35-36). Thus these words were spoken to encourage Jairus to continue to believe. He had believed in Jesus' power when his daughter was sick. He should continue to believe in Jesus' power even though his daughter was dead.

This practice of exalting Jesus' personal teaching above that through the apostles has given rise to another type of error that has resulted in many misinterpretations. The error is that of giving men's interpretation of Jesus' figurative statements greater importance than the apostles' literal statements. This is illustrated by the manner in which many people have dealt with Jesus' statements to Nicodemus. "Verily, verily, I say unto thee, Except one be born anew, he cannot see the kingdom of God" (John 3:3). "Jesus answered, Verily, verily, I say unto thee, Except one be born of water and the Spirit, he cannot enter into the kingdom of God" (John 3:5). These statements are figurative. They speak of man's becoming a child of

184 WHY DO PEOPLE NOT SEE THE BIBLE ALIKE?

God using the term commonly used to describe the process by which man became the son of Adam. They name two things from which this birth results, water and the Spirit, but give no details of how it is to come about. May we observe here, incidentally, that Nicodemus did not need to know at that time the details of entering into the kingdom of God, for the spiritual kingdom of God under the Lord Jesus Christ as king had not been established. It was only at hand. So the lesson that was in order and very important was the teaching that in order to enter the kingdom one must become a new creature, a spiritual being. As we have already seen, this spiritual kingdom was ready when Jesus was exalted to the right hand of God and made both Lord and Christ at which time the apostles, his witnesses, began to make known the details of entrance or how one can be born of water and the Spirit. Many people have rejected the straightforward, literal teaching of the apostles voiced by Peter on the day of Pentecost because they have already filled in their own details of the new birth and they fail to agree with those given by the apostles.

There is another area of the New Testament teaching in which differences of interpretation have arisen due to a failure to recognize the danger of reading one's own ideas into figurative Bible teaching. This is the book of Revelation. This is one of the most open fields for the influence of ignorance, self-deception and conceitedness and has given rise to the most radically divergent ideas. This being true, let us heed the warning of the danger of reading our ideas into figurative or symbolic statements and then distorting the teachings of our Lord to make them correspond with our ideas. Reverse the matter. Make the literal teachings of the Bible your foundation and interpret the figurative teachings in keeping therewith, or forever be ignorant of their interpretation.

Another area of New Testament teaching that has given rise to many differences is the book of the Acts of the Apostles. Many of the differences here have already been referred to but others result from the varying degrees of strictness with which the statements are interpreted. Some students of the Bible seek the exact meaning and strive to make most careful application, while others are inclined to generalize and exercise a great deal of religious freedom. At this point, we shall not take the time to show the need for most careful interpretation and most implicit application as this matter will be discussed later, but since the majority of people are inclined toward taking very wide freedom with the Word of God, it appears in order to remind you of a very strong influence among us in that direction.

In this country, whose settlement was by the people who were seeking freedom, whose government was founded upon the principle of freedom, whose most cherished ideal has been that of liberty or freedom, whose boast of superiority has been the privilege of freedom, whose plea of patriotic loyalty has been to protect and extend freedom, and whose literature and song perpetually reflect and inspire thoughts and feelings of freedom, it is not at all surprising that we have failed to recognize that every freedom is accompanied with a proportionate responsibility. In magnifying the glory of freedom, the responsibility that accompanies it has been overshadowed and become obscure. Freedom of choice should not be confused with freedom from the ultimate consequences of that choice. Freedom of religion should never be interpreted as a guarantee against the errors made in exercising that freedom. A fact that should not be overlooked is that freedom of religion, as we know it, is only a freedom of human origin and is merely a freedom from human interference. Men have only agreed that they will allow each other to worship any god he chooses, in any way he chooses, or to worship no god at all, without incurring the disfavor of the civil authorities. God has granted no such freedom. On the contrary, he has proclaimed the existence of only one God and repeatedly emphasized the one way to honor and serve him and the terrible consequences to those who reject his authority by modifying it or substituting some other.

It is true that freedom with respect to a certain activity means exemption from penalty or punishment as a result of participation in the activity, but it provides the exemption from penalty or punishment only within the realm of the authority granting the freedom. Since the real penalty or punishment for religious failures is wholly within the power of divine authority, it is a grave mistake to confuse the two and to take liberties in things that pertain to God because human agencies do not object. Care should be exercised that we do not permit ourselves to be misled by a false feeling of security by our overdrawn concept of freedom. May our human freedom which is so dearly cherished that it has become sacred, not be mistaken for divine freedom. The only true freedom in religion must be that which is granted by the only one who has authority in that field—the Almighty, the Creator of heaven and earth, the Maker of us all.

The freedom which he has granted is the freedom of choice, with a full warning of the consequences that will follow. If one chooses Jehovah to be his God and gives him the place of honor and respect by seeking wholeheartedly to know what is pleasing unto him and striving unreservedly to walk in the way of righteousness, recognizing God, and God alone, as the author of such wisdom as fills us with reverence and awe, causing all human ideas to fade into insignificance, he shall receive the blessings of this life and the glories of the life to come.

On the other hand, he that chooses some other god, or nominally chooses Jehovah but never gives him the place of full authority in his heart, disrespecting him through a lack of respect for his Word and a failure to sanctify it in his heart as a wisdom that should never be replaced by the puny ideas of man, has no promise of God's protecting care in this life and a full share of the anguish and horrors of the wicked in the eternity which follows this life.

Another source of differences of interpretation and application of New Testament teaching is found in the failure to understand the nature of Jesus' teaching. The nature of any message is determined by the source from which it comes, the one by whom it is sent and the character of the person or people to whom it is sent. A message sent to you by a friend because he is your friend and knows you to be his friend would not have the same meaning to you as the same message from someone who is not your friend, or does not know you to be his friend. These factors also determine the nature and the wording of the message that would be sent. Then let us consider the source, the purpose and the people to whom the New Testament teaching has been sent.

The source is God, and John tells us, "God is love" (I John 4:4, 16). This short, direct statement of the nature of our God should not be forgotten as we study his teaching through the Lord Jesus Christ, for this is the source of that teaching. It originated in, and emanated from, the great God of the universe and John tells us that he is love. Though we may not fully grasp the meaning of this statement about our God, surely it conveys to us the concept of one who is kind, good, helpful, and patient. He is a friend who looks upon man's waywardness with pity and tenderly extends to him a hand of mercy. Regardless of the meaning that you may attach to other terms which have been used to describe our God, there can be no doubt that our teaching originated in his love, for John also tells us,

"For God so loved the world, that he gave his only begotten Son, that whosoever believeth on him should not perish, but have eternal life" (John 3:16). Thus God sent his Son into the world to bring his teaching to us because he loved us. In this we see the love of God reaching down to his creatures making known to them their sinful condition, warning them of the consequences of sin, revealing to them his goodness and mercy, and offering unto them the way of life. So great was God's love for men that he selected as the bearer of his message not a man, not an angel, but one who partook fully of his nature, his only begotten Son. He selected one who was likewise the embodiment of love, one who could truly represent him among men, one who could not only deliver the teaching in word but could illustrate and demonstrate the teaching in his life. Thus we see that the New Testament teaching is a message of love, from a God of love, sent by a messenger of love.

To complete our picture, there is one other thing that should be considered. The message that was sent was to be interpreted and applied by those who love God, by those who believe in God, by those who want to honor God. This idea may sound strange at first, but let us examine the situation a little more closely. It is true that the world was sinful and wicked, that the people were at enmity with God, that they did not love God. But what was to happen to them before it was possible for them to accept the message of God? They must be changed from enemies to friends. They must repent of their sins against God. They must be reconciled to God. God does not honor the service of enemies but the willing service of friends. How was, and how is, the sinner brought to repentance? Paul gives us the answer in these two statements. "Or despisest thou the riches of his goodness and forbearance and longsuffering, not knowing that the goodness of God leadeth thee to repentance?" (Rom. 2:4). "For godly sorrow worketh repentance unto salvation, a repentance which bringeth no regret: but the sorrow of the world worketh death" (II Cor. 7:10). Here we are told that the "goodness of God" leads us to repentance, and that "godly sorrow worketh repentance." Putting the two statements together, it is clear that the goodness of God through godly sorrow bringeth one to repentance. Thus the goodness of God that he has extended to man even in his sinfulness and rebellion and has manifested in his love by sending his Son, when given reality through faith in God's teaching causes one to repent. One who is truly conscious of God's goodness and love toward him has his heart filled with sorrow and regret that he has treated God so shamefully and this sorrow toward God works a change in the attitude of his heart which prepares him for a change in his relationship and his attitude of life. He was an enemy of God, but his attitude has been changed. He has become reconciled. He is now a friend of God and he is ready to act like a friend, respecting and honoring his Maker. It is necessary that this change in attitude come first, before man reaches the point of accepting and applying God's teaching in his own life. And thus we see that so far as understanding the various instructions which should guide people in obedience to Christ and in their Christian living is concerned, it was to people who love God, for love is the only basis of true repentance. Punishment or the fear of punishment may cause one to cease practicing certain things and begin the practice of certain other things, but it does not change the heart in such a way as to work reconciliation. Therefore, those who have truly and sincerely accepted God's teaching to do it are those who love God. So the teaching with which we are dealing, God's teaching through Christ, is not only a message of love, from a God of love, by a messenger of love, but is to be interpreted and applied by people who love him.

In view of these facts, what should we expect to be the general character of the teaching, and what the nature of the language in which it is expressed? Should we expect our God to give us an exacting, domineering, threatening sort of teaching? A God who loves us and teaches us through his word that his children love him and that those who have not the Spirit of Christ are none of his—should we expect his teaching to be couched in such demanding terms with every failure or disobedience accompanied by a threat of punishment or destruction? Yet there are some people who make the impression that they expect to find everything God expects them to do set forth in such language as, "thou shalt do this, or be damned." When one speaks to such people of their failure in some practice of Christian living, they respond by saying, "Show me where the Bible says that I must do this or go to the place of punishment, and I will do it." Or, if they are remonstrated with for indulging in some practice that is unbecoming, they reply, "Show me where the Bible says that I must not do this and I shall quit." Such people are to be pitied. They have not only an erroneous conception of the nature of Jesus' teaching but also of the nature of Christianity, and unless it changes it is to be feared that they are already on the way toward the place to which they do not want to go.

Why should we expect God to speak to those who love him as man would speak to his slave or his prisoner? May we illustrate the matter. A guard with his gun is directing a group of men in constructing a road. The men are doing the work because they have violated the laws of society and are forced to do it as their penalty. Under such conditions, such stern and threatening language might be expected and might be necessary. Suppose, however, the construction of the same road was being done by a group of friends to honor their mutual friend and to show their love for one who had been a great friend to all of them. The director of the work is merely passing on to these people the wishes and instruction of him whom they desire so much to honor and for which work they have gladly volunteered their services. Would they expect such direct and threatening language as used in the other case? The very thought of such would be absurd.

Then why should we expect such in the instruction that God has given to them who love him and who want to honor him?

One of the causes for this is the failure of people to recognize the difference between the law of Moses and the law of Christ. As we have already observed, the law of Moses was given to a rebellious and an unfaithful people. They became subject to it by birth or nationality. At the age of eight days every male child was circumcised, which sign placed him under the law and bound him to be subject to it. He had no individual choice in the matter; otherwise he would be an outcast from his people. Thus it was necessary for a law given to such people under such conditions to be plain and emphatically set forth.

Another special need for its exactness in statement was occasioned by the fact that punishment was the principal motivating force and this was to be administered by man himself. On the other hand, the law of Christ is to all men who will believe it and who in love accept it. Each individual who is to interpret and apply this teaching in his life has accepted it voluntarily, being led to do so by the goodness of God and having no right whatsoever to administer punishment to others because of their failure to live in keeping with the teaching. Neither is he to fear punishment from others because of his own failings or transgression. The New Testament record does not leave us to depend upon the outcome of our own logic to tell us that the two teachings are very contrasting in nature.

Paul's statements leave no doubt of this. "But now we have been discharged from the law, having died to that wherein we were held; so that we serve in newness of the spirit, and not in oldness of the letter" (Rom. 7:6). "Who also made us sufficient as ministers of a new covenant; not of the letter, but of the spirit: for the letter killeth, but the spirit giveth life" (II Cor. 3:6).

We are living and serving God under the law of the spirit and we should use every care not to abuse or to distort it by dealing with it and applying it as we would the law of the letter. This may be illustrated from Jesus' teaching. He said, "Ye have heard that it was said to them of old time, Thou shalt not kill; and whosoever shall kill shall be in danger of the judgment" (Matt. 5:21). Thus the law which was to be administered by men was based upon the act itself, the actual letter of the statement. But Jesus pointed out that in his teaching it was different. "But I say unto you, that every one who is angry with his brother shall be in danger of the judgment; and whosoever shall say to his brother, Raca, shall be in danger of the council; and whosoever shall say, Thou fool, shall be in danger of the hell of fire" (Matt. 5:22). The person who was angry with his brother was subject to the same danger. Again he said, "Ye have heard that it was said, Thou shalt not commit adultery: but I say unto you, that every one that looketh on a woman to lust after her hath committed adultery with her already in his heart" (Matt. 5:27-28). Here it is clear that the old teaching, as a law of restraint to a rebellious people, was against the act itself. The new teaching puts the one who has that condition of heart and life that would lead him to commit the act, had he the opportunity, in the same class as the one who indulges in that which is a violation of God's teaching under the law of Moses. And it is evident that the spirit of Jesus' teaching must be obeyed and not merely the letter of his teaching.

This not only applies to doing those things that one ought not to do, but also to those things that Jesus has taught us to do. The Jews were taught specifically to tithe. That was a definite measure of their giving, but nowhere does the New Testament teach that we should tithe, but our giving is determined by the spirit of Christ which is within. The terms used under the law of Christ to indicate how much one should give are all general or relative. "He that giveth, let him do it with liberality" (Rom. 12:8). "But this I say, He that soweth sparingly shall reap also sparingly; and he that soweth bountifully shall reap also bountifully. Let each man do according as he hath purposed in his heart: not grudgingly, or of necessity: for God loveth a cheerful giver" (II Cor. 9:6-7). "For if the readiness is there, it is acceptable according as a man hath, not according as he hath not" (II Cor. 8:12). And so it is with many of the teachings that Jesus has given unto us. We have been told how we can please God, how we can honor him, but the exact bounds have not been marked out, the exact demands have not been stated, as to how much we should do or how frequently we should do those things. We are shown that attending church and praising God is acceptable but we are not told that we must attend worship with a certain frequency. We are taught that we should study God's Word, but there is no definite commandment as to the amount. We are told to sing with the spirit and with the understanding, but no quantity or bound is set. We are told to pray with the spirit and with the understanding, how to pray and many other things about prayer, but all terms that refer to frequency are general terms. Even when Jesus gave the Supper, he gave no definite statement as to the frequency with which it should be partaken of, but he made it clear as to how it was to be partaken of, and for what purpose. But the frequency of this sacred practice (apostolic example indicates the first day of the week) is determined by the spirit of Christ which is within. And Paul tells us, "But if any man hath not the Spirit of Christ, he is none of his" (Rom. 8:9). All of this does not mean that under the New Testament teaching our obligation is less, instead it is greater. Neither does this in anywise suggest that we are more at liberty to ignore God's wishes and substitute our own ideas or to generally do as we please and be pleasing unto God than the people could who lived under the old law. In one sense, we are left to do as we please, but the spirit of Christ only pleases to do one way and that is the way that honors and glorifies God.

The practice of dealing with the New Testament teaching as a law of the letter has also been encouraged by a method of teaching or a method of testing religious activities. It is the method of insisting upon a chapter and verse citation or a "thus saith the Lord" for everything practiced in religion. The method appears to be very praise-worthy, the underlying principle is unmistakably sound and the goal sought—loyalty to God's authority—is certainly above question. However, a prolonged and growing emphasis upon "you are commanded to do this" and "you are commanded not to do that," or "you are not commanded to do that" without due emphasis upon the basic Bible teaching and the spiritual nature of the New Testament teaching to give a fully balanced perspective has had a narrowing and, hence, a distorting effect upon interpretation. Through this influence some people have become legalists, considering themselves righteous for having complied with a limited number of tenets particularly stressed by their own religious group and feeling free to indulge in many activities contrary to the spirit of the teaching because there is no literal prohibition. They also excuse themselves from many good works because they have found no specific commandment ordering such.

It is hoped that this statement will not be misunderstood. We must respect the authority of God's Word implicitly. We cannot afford either to add to it or to take from it. Neither can we afford to obscure its true meaning.

This practice of expecting all questions to be answered by direct quotations has encouraged a conception of the New Testament teaching that is overly-simplified. It has caused many people to overlook the fact that the New Testament teaching is a complex system of thought and like all other complex systems of thought only the simple and easy questions are answered that way. The more difficult questions are to be answered by the application of principle and can be answered correctly only out of a wealth of information and experience in the teaching itself. Some people seem to think that anyone ought to be able to take a few correct references on any question, read the Bible for a little while, and find the correct answer regardless of his spiritual background. This is the case only with questions for which direct answers are given and is very uncertain even then due to human prejudices.

This may be done with questions of this sort in other fields. For example, some of the simpler questions in chemistry, physics, or medicine may be answered, by an intelligent person, by reading the right book and the right page, even though he has not studied the field. But the difficult questions will be answered only by the person who has studied and also has had fruitful experience in the field. That this is true in regard to understanding instruction on spiritual things (or Bible teaching) the writer of Hebrews leaves no doubt. After speaking of Christ's having been "named of God a high priest after the order of Melchizedek" (Heb. 5:10) he states, "Of whom we have many things to say, and hard of interpretation, seeing ye are become dull of hearing.

For when by reason of the time ye ought to be teachers, ye have need again that some one teach you the rudiments of the first principles of the oracles of God; and are become such as have need of milk, and not of solid food. For every one that partaketh of milk is without experience of the word of righteousness; for he is a babe. But solid food is for fullgrown men, even those who by reason of use have their senses exercised to discern good and evil" (Heb. 5:11-14). This failure to grow, this failure to exercise their senses to discern good and evil, this being without experience of the word of righteousness caused the teaching to be hard of interpretation. Furthermore, Peter speaks of some things written by Paul being hard to be understood and tells us what the ignorant and unsteadfast (spiritually weak or unstable) do with them. "And account that the longsuffering of our Lord is salvation; even as our beloved brother Paul also, according to the wisdom given to him, wrote unto you; as also in all his epistles, speaking in them of these things; wherein are some things hard to be understood, which the ignorant and unsteadfast wrest, as they do also the other scriptures, unto their own destruction" (II Pet. 3:15-16).

This should in nowise justify any human being in his failure to study the Bible for himself any more than the fact that a third grade pupil's inability to understand higher mathematics would justify his refusal to study arithmetic. However, it should sap our conceitedness a bit and cause us to be slow in becoming over-confident in feeling that we have all of the an-

swers and that they are unquestionably correct. Many
have been the preachers who have taught things in
their early preaching that they would not preach after
they had learned more. And the Lord only knows
how many ought to learn better than to teach some of
the things being taught today. We should remember
that the person who is puffed up over his knowledge,
"knoweth not yet as he ought to know" (I Cor. 8:2).
Even in the fields of human knowledge, it is the little
man who boasts of his knowledge. The person who
is well trained recognizes there is so much he does not
know that he is humble in his attitude toward it.

How much more true should this be of those who are
teachers of the Bible, on some questions especially, since
all of the answers are not revealed. In all kindness may
I say that probably one of the greatest sources of differences on Bible teaching is to be found in the reck-
lessness with which unanswered questions are answered
(?) by people who feel that the failure to answer would
be detrimental to their prestige.

I pray God that we may recognize the true relationship between the personal teaching of John and Jesus
and Jesus' teaching through the apostles guided by the
Holy Spirit. Also I pray that we may learn the true
nature of God's teaching to us that we may understand
its meaning and not allow it to be obscured either by
our personal weaknesses or our methods of teaching.
May we have the spirit of Christ and seek to honor God
by following his example.

QUESTIONS ON LECTURE XII

1. Give further evidence that we are to hear Jesus and not Moses as a law giver.
2. What people were never under the law of Moses?
3. What did Paul say that anyone who taught the people to turn to the law was doing to the gospel?
4. Give the two sub-divisions of the period of reconciliation.
5. What part of the New Testament teaching does each include?
6. How did John show recognition of the temporary nature of his work?
7. In order for the blessings of Abraham to come upon the Gentiles, what had to take place?
8. At what time did the actual fulfillment of the promise made to Abraham that all nations would be blessed through his seed begin?
9. What is one of the principal sources of religious differences in this part of the Bible record?
10. What particular practice in regard to the personal teaching of Jesus has given rise to misunderstandings and differences?
11. "Fear not, only believe" was never said in Bible record in answer to what question?
12. For what purpose were these words spoken?
13. What figurative language of Jesus has been put above literal teachings by his apostles in following the practice mentioned in question ten?
14. What other figurative language in the New Testament has in a similar manner given rise to many religious differences?
15. What has caused many differences of interpretation of the teachings in the book of Acts?
16. Show how the American idea of freedom may be influencing our Bible interpretation.
17. What is the only real source of religious freedom?
18. What is the freedom and upon what grounds is it granted?
19. What is the nature of the source of the New Testament teaching, the messenger who brought it and the teaching itself?

20. Carefully show the character of the people who are to interpret and apply the New Testament teaching.
21. Contrast punishment and love as motives.
22. Show why people should not expect demanding, threatening language in the New Testament teaching.
23. Contrast the law of Moses and the law of Christ as to purpose, people and nature.
24. Carefully illustrate the difference in the natures of the two laws.
25. What practice today has tended to make some people legalists?
26. What other effect has the practice of expecting all questions to be answered by direct quotation encouraged?
27. Show how that experience in study and living is necessary to the proper understanding of much of God's teaching.
28. What should the fact that some of God's teaching is difficult of interpretation not justify, but what effect should it have upon those who study it?
29. What is a great source of religious differences related to the fact that the Bible does not answer all of the questions?

LECTURE XIII

WHY DO PEOPLE NOT STUDY THE BIBLE?

IN an earlier study of "Why Do People Not See the Bible Alike," it has been suggested that people who are ignorant of God's word may be classified into two groups: those who have studied, and those who have not studied. To the present, we have been primarily concerned with the first group. We shall now consider the second group, those who have not studied the Bible. On a less important question this would be thought unnecessary as people would generally conclude that the fact that one does not study is sufficient reason for one not understanding or agreeing upon a teaching. However, since so many people, even among those who call themselves Christians, do not really study the Bible, and since it is the teaching upon which their future destiny depends, one feels compelled to seek a more analytical answer with a prayer that some may be caused to weigh the matter and be aroused from their present state of indifference. So our question now becomes, "Why Do People Not Study the Bible?"

Were this question made personal to a large number of people, a wide variety of statements would be made in reply, but very few of them would name real causes. However, it is very likely that most of the replies would be expressions of self-defense or justification, all of which imply the same cause. That cause or reason frankly expressed would be "I do not really want to study the Bible." To this attitude there are probably several contributing factors but we shall consider only three as being basic, and they are very closely inter-linked. They are: the nature of study, the failure to recognize the great blessings in Bible study, and the lack of a conviction of the necessity for Bible study. Now let us weigh these in this order.

Study is work, real work. It does not merely require time, but demands human energy, mental energy, which is the highest form of energy. The real study in any field is done by the minority of the people. Then the results are used by others. This is a universal practice. So in the field of religion most people want ready-made answers to their questions. It is habitual. And since they make very little use of Bible ideas even in conversation and seldom put them to a rigid test, they appear to suffer no real handicap or embarrassment from the practice. They even have the comfort of the majority. Among their associates, ignorance of the Bible is readily excused and frequently passed over with a pleasantry that almost commends it. Should the situation be such as to imply some failure to meet personal responsibility, the differences that exist among those who have studied the Bible are pointed to as evidence of the difficulty in understanding it and offered as full justification for lack of study.

Our second and third reasons why people do not want to study the Bible—the failure to recognize the great blessings in Bible study, and the lack of a conviction of the necessity for Bible study—are very closely related in that they combine in effectively robbing one of all real motivation for Bible study. In fact, they constitute the real causes of failure, the difficulty of study only serving to make them the more important. If the reward we see is sufficiently great and the need is imperative, the difficulty of the task becomes a minor factor.

The failure to recognize the great blessings in Bible study is the result of a failure to learn two important lessons from the Bible: the Word of God can save our souls, and the Word of God is our guide to success and happiness in this world. James admonished, "Wherefore putting away all filthiness and overflowing of wickedness, receive with meekness the implanted word, which is able to save your souls" (Jas. 1:21). We should note here that the Word must be implanted or ingrafted, which can only result from study. Paul said to the elders of the church at Ephesus, "And now I commend you to God, and to the word of his grace, which is able to build you up, and to give you the inheritance among all them that are sanctified" (Acts 20:32). Peter urged, "Putting away therefore all wickedness, and all guile, and hypocrisies, and envies, and all evil speakings, as newborn babes, long for the spiritual milk which is without guile, that ye may grow thereby unto salvation" (I Pet. 2:1-2). If we "long for the spiritual milk," or "sincere milk of the word" as expressed in the King James version, we certainly will seek to know the teaching by the normal method, study. Peter also declared that, "Seeing that his divine power hath granted unto us all things that pertain unto life and godliness, through the knowledge of him that called us by his own glory and virtue" (II Pet. 1:3). Can we take these statements seriously and not make an honest effort to make God's Word a lamp unto our feet and a light unto our path as did David? (Ps. 119: 105)

We should not stress the ultimate goal, however, and slight the rewards to be enjoyed here and now. In fact, if we fail to secure the earthly fruits of the seed of the kingdom, we need not hope for the eternal. Jesus said, "But seek ye first his kingdom and his righteousness; and all these things shall be added unto you" (Matt. 6:33). How can we truly seek his kingdom and his righteousness and not study the book that tells us how to do it? David has shown us that the man who loves and studies God's Word will prosper. "Blessed is the man that walketh not in the counsel of the wicked, Nor standeth in the way of sinners, Nor sitteth in the seat of scoffers: But his delight is in the law of Jehovah; and on his law doth he meditate day and night. And he shall be like a tree planted by the streams of water, That bringeth forth its fruit in its season, Whose leaf also doth not wither; And whatsoever he doeth shall prosper" (Ps. 1:1-3).

Not only is the Bible a guide to temporal blessings, but also the only true guide to happiness as well. Paul exhorted, "Rejoice in the Lord always: again I will say, Rejoice" (Phil. 4:4). The early Christians showed

this joy in their lives despite their sufferings and persecutions. We find people today seeking happiness or
the solution to their problems through the sociologist
or psychologist only because they have failed to seek
the daily guidance of God's Word. Do you want a
guide to happiness? Turn to your Bible and study.
Do you want your burdens lightened? Go to your
Bible. Do you want the best principles of health? Find
them in your Bible. Do you want to avoid personal
conflicts or adjust personal problems? Learn your
Bible. Do you want to be the right kind of son or
daughter, brother or sister, husband or wife, father or
mother, teacher or student, employer or employee?
Study your Bible. Do you want to learn to love others
or want people to love you? Practice your Bible.

The lack of a conviction of the necessity for Bible
study is due to a failure to learn one of the basic lessons
of the Bible, a lesson that has been taught most
thoroughly. It is taught from the early record of
Genesis to the last chapter in Revelation. Briefly
stated the lesson is this: man's honor and respect for
God can only be shown by honoring and respecting
his Word.

It is not a matter of how great a thing man may do,
how much sacrifice he may make, or how much persecution he may suffer, but rather how implicitly he
puts his trust in God and with what humility he en-
thrones God in his heart, giving him the complete rule
over his life, doing honor to the wisdom of God by the
care with which he follows his teaching. The record

of God's dealing with man through the ages abounds in cases that illustrate this lesson. On many occasions where man did the will of his Father implicitly he received God's blessings, and on many occasions where he fell short of implicit obedience he suffered for it. We shall carefully review a few of the cases of the latter type since they provide a more graphic illustration of the fact that man incurs the disfavor of his Maker whenever he disrespects his word in any way.

This was the cause of man's trouble in the garden of Eden. When God had made man, we are told that, "And Jehovah God took the man, and put him into the Garden of Eden to dress it and to keep it. And Jehovah God commanded the man, saying, Of every tree of the garden thou mayest freely eat: but of the tree of the knowledge of good and evil, thou shalt not eat of it: for in the day that thou eatest thereof thou shalt surely die" (Gen. 2:15-17). Here we learn that God gave man a two-fold instruction: he was to dress and keep the garden, and he was not to eat of the tree of the knowledge of good and evil. So far as our record indicates, man complied with the first instruction fully. There is no implication that he failed in the work that he was to do, but he failed to respect God in regard to that which he was not to do.

Everyone is acquainted with the story of Eve's temptation. She knew God's instruction in the matter. She knew that God had told them not to eat of the fruit of the tree of the knowledge of good and evil; but she was not willing to leave the matter, accepting God's way as best. The fact that God had spoken was not enough. She ignored his instruction and began to weigh the matter for herself. Eve resorted to her own thinking in the matter, and was soon led to ignore God's teaching. This was her fatal mistake and one that is still being made by many among her posterity. She proposed to weigh the facts for herself. She did. She arrived at her own decision, one that dishonored and dethroned God. The facts given her in regard to the fruit were absolutely correct. It was good food. It was a delight to the eyes. And, it would make her wise to know good and evil. As she thought of these things and was reminded that God knew that it would cause her to know good and evil, and surely she would not die for doing a thing like that, she seems to have come to the conclusion that her Creator and Maker would not do what he said he would. So she disrespected his teaching. She dethroned her God and enthroned her reason, a thing that man has been doing from that day until this. And how frequently do we hear people today justify some practice in rejecting some portion of God's Word after the same fashion? How often do people reason today that "this is just a little thing," admitting that they are not following the will of God in its strictest interpretation but reasoning that "surely this will be all right," or "this is just as good." Surely one who justifies his accepting a teaching this way does not recognize the seriousness of his act. Surely he does not really mean what he is saying. What does the saying "this is just as good" really mean? What is just as good as what? It means that man's idea is just as good as God's teaching on the point in question, that man's wisdom is just as good as God's wisdom. Probably Eve thought the same thing but what a mistake!

Have we ever fully considered what Eve really did in the light of human reasoning. She did not repudiate God. She did not deny that he was God. She did not refuse to worship him as God. She did not blaspheme his name. She did not become a moral degenerate. What did she do? She took a piece of fruit and ate it. She did not steal from a neighbor. She did not shed the blood of her fellow man. She did not bear false witness. She did not lie. She merely took a piece of fruit and ate it and gave to her husband with her and he ate. Can we think of an act that is less offensive? Can we think of an act that would appear to be less degrading? Then why was this such a terrible thing to do? Do we ever hear such a question asked today? The magnitude of this wrong cannot be measured by the human evaluation of the act itself. It can only be measured correctly when God's Word is taken into consideration. From that standpoint, what had she done? She had replaced God's teaching by her own decision in the matter, and in so doing, she had dethroned God and enthroned herself, or her judgment. When man exalts his human wisdom above the authority of his Maker, he has done a terrible thing, a thing that is an insult to his God. Because of this act, that very day man was separated from God, driven out into a world that was cursed because of him, a world in which he was destined to lose that place of honor that his Maker assigned to him when he set him over the works of his hand.

Now since God drove man out from his presence because man dishonored his word, why should we expect God to take us back until we have enthroned him in our heart completely, until we are willing to follow his word implicitly, until we are willing to honor him in humility, by seeking to know what he would have us to do and exercising the greatest care to do it the best we can? We should not forget that he only asks to be our God. Someone might ask, "Is he not God? Do not people call him God?" He is not our God until we treat him as God, not merely call him God. He is our God only when we enthrone him in our life to rule over it.

But someone may object, "This teaching about Eve is Old Testament teaching. We are living under the teachings through Christ." This is a true statement. At least, the facts stated are correct, but the implication is false. This principle has not changed. The only way that man can honor God today is through implicit obedience to his will. The teaching which God has given us through the Lord Jesus Christ must be respected as fully and as carefully as the teaching which God gave to Adam in person, or that which he gave to the people of Israel through Moses.

Jesus made this plain at the time of his temptation. In the very first recorded statement made after the time of his baptism he taught this very lesson. When Satan challenged his sonship by asking that he change the stones to bread, our Saviour answered with a teaching that had been given before this time but was still to be respected. "But he answered and said, It is written, Man shall not live by bread alone, but by every word that proceedeth out of the mouth of God" (Matt. 4:4). Moses had given this teaching in the long ago (Deut. 8:3). It is just as true today. Man shall live by every word that proceedeth out of the mouth of God. This Adam and Eve failed to do, so they were cut off from the tree of life and they ceased to live. And so will it be with us. If we refuse to honor completely and fully all of God's teaching that he has revealed to us through the Lord Jesus Christ, which teaching includes all of the basic lessons of the Bible as a whole, we should not expect to return to that close relationship with God that man had in the beginning. Since God drove man out from that close association because he refused to respect his word, why should we think that he will receive man back into that close relationship to dwell for eternity when man has not learned to respect his word. This does not necessarily imply that God expects of man perfection, that he expects man to make no mistake, but he does expect man to enthrone him as God, and impelled by the love shown through the Lord Jesus Christ, to live "unto him who for their sakes died and rose again."

It was in the last days of the life of Moses when he gathered the people in the land of Moab and gave to them his final message that he reminded them that

God had humbled them and suffered them to hunger
and fed them with manna, "that he might make thee
know that man doth not live by bread only, but by
everything that proceedeth out of the mouth of Jehovah
doth man live" (Deut. 8:3).   On that same occasion he
solemnly charged them, "Ye shall not add unto the word
which I command you, neither shall ye diminish from
it, that ye may keep the commandments of Jehovah
your God which I command you" (Deut. 4:2).   With
what a bitter experience Moses had learned the weight
of these words.   It was in the wilderness of Zin at
the water of Meribah where the people strove with
Moses because they had no water.   "And Jehovah spake
unto Moses, saying, Take the rod, and assemble the
congregation, thou, and Aaron thy brother, and speak
ye unto the rock before their eyes, that it give forth
its water; and thou shalt bring forth to them water out
of the rock; so thou shalt give the congregation and
their cattle drink.   And Moses took the rod from before
Jehovah, as he commanded him.   And Moses and
Aaron gathered the assembly together before the rock,
and he said unto them, Hear now, ye rebels; shall we
bring you forth water out of this rock?   And Moses
lifted up his hand, and smote the rock with his rod
twice: and water came forth abundantly, and the congregation drank, and their cattle.   And Jehovah said
unto Moses and Aaron, Because ye believed not in me,
to sanctify me in the eyes of the children of Israel,
therefore ye shall not bring this assembly into the land
which I have given them" (Num. 20:7-12).

Moses reminded the people of this experience and told them that he had prayed to God that he might go over the Jordan, but had been told that he must die in the land of Moab. Why should this Moses who had led the people of Israel for nearly forty years be refused admission to the land of Canaan? This question is answered by Jehovah himself when he announced to Moses and Aaron at Mount Hor that the time had come for Aaron to be gathered unto his people, for neither was he permitted to enter into the land of Canaan because of this disobedience. God said, "Because ye rebelled against my word at the waters of Meribah" (Num. 20:24).

Now let us view a few other Old Testament happenings that illustrate further how easy it is for man to reject God. When Samuel was old and his sons who were serving as judges over Israel had become wicked, the people came to Samuel with the request that he give them a king. They knew that was not God's order of things and Samuel pled with them to turn away from the idea. Samuel took the matter to Jehovah. "And Jehovah said unto Samuel, Hearken unto the voice of the people in all that they say unto thee; for they have not rejected thee, but they have rejected me, that I should not be king over them" (I Sam. 8:7). This was not an announcement by the people that they would no longer worship God. This was not a declaration that they were discarding the tabernacle worship. This was not a confession that they no longer believed in God. Yet God says, "They have rejected me, that I should not be king over them." They had set aside one item in God's arrangement. They had dethroned God and enthroned their own wisdom. Doubtless they would have denied rejecting God, just as some people take a similar liberty with the teaching of Jehovah today but still claim to serve him and be faithful to him.

We have a similar example in the reign of the very first king of Israel. Through Samuel, God declared unto Saul that the Amalekites should be utterly destroyed because they had fought against Israel while the people were on their way from Egypt to the land of Canaan. So he said to Saul, "Now go and smite Amalek, and utterly destroy all that they have, and spare them not; but slay both man and woman, infant and suckling, ox and sheep, camel and ass" (I Sam. 15:3). We are told that Saul gathered an army of two hundred and ten thousand men and warned the Kenites to separate themselves from the Amalekites. He slew the Amalekites, man, woman and child, with the exception of one man, king Agag. He destroyed all of the sheep and oxen, the fatlings and the lambs, with the exception of a few. He brought them and king Agag back home with him. When he met Samuel, Saul said, "I have performed the commandment of Jehovah. And Samuel said, What meaneth then this bleating of the sheep in mine ears, and the lowing of the oxen which I hear?" (I Sam. 15:13-14).

Were we to measure what Saul did by the human measure that we sometimes want to apply to matters of Christianity, we would probably conclude that king Saul did extra well. He gathered a large army, separated the people, destroyed all but one, and all but a very few cattle. In fact, for all "practical purposes" as Saul expressed it he "performed the commandments of God." Yet Samuel said, "Because thou hast rejected the word of Jehovah, he hath also rejected thee from being king" (I Sam. 15:23). Had it been something that Saul could not do it would have been different. But it was something that Saul could do but would not. This is the sort of thing that shows without question that one has dethroned God.

Here we are reminded of the graphic manner in which Jesus expressed the same lesson. "And why call ye me, Lord, Lord, and do not the things which I say?" (Luke 6:46). Lord means ruler. To call him Lord and not submit to his teaching was a case of their actions belying their words, the gravest sort of inconsistency.

As our last case in point, we turn to the history of Jeroboam. He had led the people away from the worship of God in Jerusalem and built altars at Dan and Bethel. He was worshiping at the altar at Bethel when a man of God out of Judah came to cry against the altar. God had told this man from Judah to go to Bethel and cry against this altar, not to eat anything while he was in that country, and to return by another way. The man of Judah was courageous. He did not fear to face king Jeroboam. He fully delivered his message against the altar. When Jeroboam put forth his hand against the man of God from Judah it dried up. Also, the altar was rent and the ashes poured out, which was the sign that God had given to the man of God. Jeroboam entreated him to ask the favor of Jehovah and restore his hand. The man of God from Judah did so, showing that the power of God was with him. Jeroboam invited the man to go home with him to refresh himself and receive a reward, but received the answer that he would not even for half of Jeroboam's house, and explained that God had told him not to eat in that country. The man of God from Judah started on his return journey according to his instructions, by another way. But when an old prophet who lived in that country heard of the matter, he pursued the man of God and overtook him. He found him sitting under an oak. He invited the man of God to go home with him to dinner, but was refused and was given the reason why. But the old prophet said, "I also am a prophet as thou art; and an angel spake unto me by the word of Jehovah, saying, Bring him back with thee into thy house, that he may eat bread and drink water. But he lied unto him" (I Kings 13:18). So the man of God went back with the old prophet. While they sat at the table, the word of God did come to the old prophet and the message was to the man of God from Judah, "Forasmuch as thou hast been disobedient unto the mouth of Jehovah, and hast not kept the commandment which Jehovah thy God commanded thee, but camest back, and hast eaten bread and drunk water in the place of which he said to thee, Eat no bread, and drink no water; thy body shall not come unto the sepulchre of thy fathers" (I Kings 13:21-22). As the man of God from Judah started on the way home a lion met him by the way and slew him. And when the old prophet came to the place where he lay, he mourned over him saying, "Alas, my brother!" (I Kings 13:30).

Why did the man of God from Judah meet such a fate? Was it because he was unwilling to do what God told him to do? Certainly not. Was it because he was afraid to go to the place where God wanted him to go? Not at all. Was it because he feared to pronounce the curse upon the altar in the presence of Jeroboam? Emphatically, no. Was it because he had forgotten part of what Jehovah had told him to do? Not in the least. It was because he was willing to listen to man instead of following God's word implicitly. He listened to a man who came to him as a prophet of God, who evidently was well respected in the community and who claimed that God had spoken unto him. But all of this did not excuse the man of God. Neither will God excuse us today when we allow ourselves to be led away from the truth by men, even though they are men who are held in high esteem, who are spoken of as religious men, even by some as godly men.

Why do we allow men to stand between us and our God? Why do we allow men to turn us away from the true teaching of God? Why did God reveal himself unto man through the labors and sufferings of so many people including those of his only begotten Son? And why, through his divine providence, by the power of the Holy Spirit, has he provided us with detailed records and instructions if they are not necessary to our welfare? Why did a loving God ruthlessly drive man out from him into a world that was cursed for his sake and leave record of the same if he did not do it to teach man the need of implicit obedience? Why did he lead Moses upon Nebo's lonely mountain side in the solemn solitude of nature, from Pisgah's height, show him the land into which he was not permitted to enter, close his eyes in the sleep of death and bury him in a valley in the land of Moab? Why was this Moses whose eye was undimmed and whose natural force was not abated, who had patiently toiled and struggled with a rebellious people for forty years, who had faithfully followed God's instructions with only one exception, not permitted to enter into that land that flowed with milk and honey? Why did the God of wisdom do this thing, and why did he record it for our learning if he did not do it to teach men to respect every word that cometh from the mouth of God? Why did God record for us the story of the man of God from Judah who faithfully cried out against the altar at Bethel, who faithfully refused to dine with Jeroboam, who faithfully started on his return journey by a different route and only failed when he was led astray by the one who called himself "the prophet of God," for which he failed to return to his home and to his people, if he did not record it to warn man against the danger of being misled by men and impressing us with the need of a knowledge of the teaching of our God?

It appears only reasonable to think that one who loves God with all of his heart, with all of his soul, with all of his strength, and with all of his mind would earnestly seek to learn of God and to learn how he might truly show his love for God. Why do we forget that Jesus said, "He that loveth father or mother more than me is not worthy of me; and he that loveth son or daughter more than me is not worthy of me" (Matt. 10:37).

Someone has spoken of the epistles of the New Testament as God's love letters to the churches. It appears just as much in order to speak of the Gospels as God's love letters to the world. And if we can come to see it in its entirety, to speak of the Bible as God's love letters to man, then why has man, in view of all this, not wanted to study the Bible? Because he has not been taught to study it. In fact, he has been taught not to study it. In some cases this is true literally; in others, it has been done by example. The people who call themselves Christians who have really studied their Bibles as they did their arithmetic, are so much in the minority that the weight of example is against, instead of for studying the Bible.

Religious leaders in their teaching in their respective groups have selected a few tenets and have preached loud and long, "you must do this" and "you must not do that." But for the most part, the most important thing of all has not been included among the "musts."

If one has in mind eternal life when he asks the question, "What must I do to be saved?" and is one who has the normal life period before him, he has just as much reason to ask, "Must I study the Bible to be saved?" as he has to ask, "Must I be baptized to be saved?" "Must I attend church to be saved?" or "Must I love my neighbor to be saved?" We have no right to emphasize Peter's statement, "Repent ye, and be baptized everyone of you in the name of Jesus Christ unto the remission of your sins" (Acts 2:38), and neglect his statement, "As new born babes, long for the spiritual milk which is without guile, that ye may grow thereby unto salvation" (I Pet. 2:2). In the first statement we frequently hear emphasized "unto the remission of your sins," to show that repentance and baptism are necessary. In the second, we should put the same emphasis upon "unto salvation," to show that growth through the Word of God is necessary.

Studying God's Word is not only one way to show love for God, but it is the most natural way to show our love for God and the one way that people who love God will show it if they are properly taught. This is the surest indication that we have enthroned God in our heart. A lack of a conviction of this need is the real cause for people not wanting to study the Bible and, hence, for their failure to study the Bible. So let us not forget the lesson as Jesus taught it at the house of Mary, Martha and Lazarus (Luke 10:38-42). The one thing that man needs is to sit at Jesus' feet and hear his word.

QUESTIONS ON LECTURE XIII

1. Why should this question be given careful consideration?
2. What is the real cause frankly stated?
3. What three reasons are given for people not wanting to study the Bible?
4. What is sometimes given as an alibi for not studying the Bible?
5. Which two reasons for not wanting to study the Bible are more vital and why?
6. Give evidences that Bible study is important to one's salvation.
7. What temporal blessings may one receive from studying the Bible?
8. A lack of a conviction of the necessity for Bible study indicates the failure to learn what great Bible lesson?
9. Name some cases from the Old Testament which indicate that God required implicit obedience.
10. Analyze Eve's sin and show just what happened.
11. Give the lesson as Jesus taught it at the time of his temptation.
12. Upon what occasion did Moses learn this lesson?
13. Tell how the children of Israel rejected God in the days of Samuel.
14. Just what did Saul do, or fail to do, in rejecting God?
15. What warning should we take from the fate of the man of God from Judah who cried against Jeroboam's altar?
16. What two ways has man been taught not to study the Bible?
17. What teaching of the apostle Peter has beeen neglected?
18. What is the real cause for people not wanting to study the Bible?

An Open Letter

DEAR READER,

Whoever you are, wherever you live, whatever your religious conviction, however much you may like or dislike what you have read, I beg of you not to close this book with a comment, favorable or unfavorable, and close your eyes to the conditions that surround you —yea, the possible danger within your own life.

Surely it is evident that the purpose in studying this question is not to condemn any religious people as a group nor to justify any religious people as a group, but rather if possible to make every reader conscious of the source of his own personal danger. So I beg you to remember that we stand or fall before our Creator as individuals. We are all human beings and heir to the common human weaknesses. Some are ignorant and deceived in regard to some Bible teachings and some in regard to other Bible teachings. These have resulted in differences both individual and group or church. Far be it from me to presume to judge which differences are worse. Both or either indicates a disrespect for God's Word—a failure of many to earnestly and prayerfully study it with that degree of humility and consecration necessary to guard against human adulteration. Thus, my plea to you whether non-church member, church member, deacon, elder, preacher, or priest, soften your crust of pride and self-conceitedness enough to recognize the fact that some of your religious ideas were accepted through incidental or accidental contact with God's Word or from the teaching of some man; resolve that you will honor God by learning his Word for yourself, and study it as you have never studied before. Pray fervently and repeatedly that you may lay aside all colored glasses and see the teaching of God as it is. What everyone needs is what the Bible says and not what some man or men think it says. Be willing to honestly consider ideas that do not agree with your own, weighing them not by those that you have formerly held but by the Bible itself.

Is there anything unfair or unreasonable in this plea? You are not being asked to do something for me, to believe what I say or to join any particular church group but to prayerfully and honestly seek a true understanding of the teaching of Almighty God in the interest of your own soul and to the honor of your Creator.

This personal, individual, private Bible study is the only hope for a way out of the present religious confusion and chaos. May God bless you with a conviction that you can do something and that you should do something.

With a prayer for greater humility and service.

J. Ridley Stroop

Printed in the United States
95276LV00002B/151/A